DIVINE HAND AT WORK

Aloysius Aseervatham

ISBN: 978-1-964462-53-0 (sc)
ISBN: 978-1-964462-54-7 (e)

Rev. date: 07/10/2024

DIVINE HAND AT WORK

Aloysius Aseervatham

PREFACE

Belief in God is a deeply personal concept, one that naturally leads to contemplation on if or how God acts to help us through challenging periods of our lives. Some of us are fortunate to be allowed the opportunity to recognise God's influence on the outcome of our lives; testimonies by these 'witnesses' can hearten others who may be struggling.

In this book I have documented a selection of events, from my own life, and from those of close friends and relatives, that could be interpreted as examples of God's influence on our lives. A common theme through all these recollections is the willingness to give praise and thanks to God for being present to guide us especially through the most difficult times.

Throughout my life I have gained much knowledge and understanding from reading the life stories of holy men and women. I have included some of the stories that have particularly helped me, especially with regard to the recognition that we all have the potential to do God's work, regardless of our station in life.

I hope the stories that follow inspire you to share your own experiences with those around you, and together we will help each other move closer to living the life that God intended for us.

ACKNOWLEDGEMENT

I would like to express my sincere thanks to all those who readily contributed their experience of divine intervention at trying times in their lives.

My work on this book would not have been completed satisfactorily without the enthusiastic help from Grace Rutty of Darra-Jindalee Catholic Parish, Brisbane who having read each story wrote a concise and appropriate "Conversing with God" section.

I am grateful to my son Ratna Aseervatham for the advice and editing he so readily provided despite his busy schedule.

A special thanks goes to Pastor Lester Reinbott of Corinda, Brisbane for his willing and able theological assistance and to Augustine Mariaratnam of London, UK for providing appropriate "meditation" material for each chapter.

Last but not least, I am indebted to Chandra Perera of Brisbane for formatting this book as efficiently as she had done with a couple of my previous books.

Lourdes G

DIVINE INTERVENTION IN MY LIFE

AN EVER PRESENT HELP

God knows that we all face deep needs and troubles at various times in our lives. We also encounter turmoil, temptations and times of confusion.

God has promised us that in times of trouble He will be our ever-present help.

The phrase "ever present" means "always here, always available, with unlimited access." In short, the abiding presence of the Lord is always in us. And if he's ever-present in us, then he desires continual conversation with us. He wants us to converse with him no matter where we are: on the job, with family, with friends, even with non-believers.

God's help comes in the gift of his Holy Spirit, who dwells in us and works the Father's will in our lives.

We may think that we have to work up some emotion in order to hear from God. It is not so. He says he abides in us night and day.

If we acknowledge God in all our ways He shall direct our paths" (Proverbs 3:6).*

Psalm 46:11 **describes God's ever-present strength, his help in time of trouble, and his peace in the midst of chaos. God's presence is with us at all times, and his help always arrives when we need it.

God is always with us hearing our cries for help. He is always with us protecting us from danger. The testimonies in this book are meant to provide evidence to this fact.

A WONDERFUL PLAN

God has a wonderful plan for each of us. But since temptation, sin and evil spirits loom in this world, he knows that we will experience times of rejoicing and times of sadness and difficulty. Still, he wants us to 'rejoice always' in good times and bad times (Philippians 4:4).

God wants us to rejoice because we can experience his peace at work in us, no matter what happens.

Whenever we face happy times we should sit back and enjoy and relish them. And when we face tough times we must remember that Jesus himself suffered.

And because Jesus suffered he knows our sufferings first hand. He suffers with us and is always with us, offering his consolation and strength.

This is a great promise of Christian life. We can do all things through Christ who strengthens us. We will navigate even the most turbulent waters of life far more peacefully and successfully because Jesus is with us, helping us to do what we could never accomplish on our own.

GOD'S WORK ON HIS KINGDOM

God's Kingdom is truly among us but is not yet fully visible. He is asking us to exercise our faith and trust in his unseen presence and his invisible power.

The three main branches of Christianity: Eastern Orthodoxy (which is chiefly practiced in Russia and Eastern European countries), Roman Catholicism, and Protestantism are continuously working to bring God's Kingdom to earth. All Roman Catholic churches have the same beliefs, form, and structure but those of Protestant denominations vary depending on whether they are Episcopalians, Lutherans, Methodists, Presbyterians, Baptists, Pentecostals, or one of numerous other groups.

Jesus' humble coming in the flesh was the inauguration of God's Kingdom and that was a very quiet beginning. The Kingdom's forces are now at work in a new way but is not yet fully visible.

God is always at work in the world around us. The coming of His Kingdom is not accompanied with a lot of fanfare and many don't notice it.

1

JESUS THE GOOD SHEPHERD

"I am the good shepherd. The good shepherd lays down his life for the sheep".

The scripture says that Jesus as a good and loving shepherd keeps His sheep, those who know His voice and who listens for His voice, under his care. When His sheep wander away and get into trouble He is there to look for them and take them back and shower his love. They belong to him and he belongs to them.

When I was a child, I was dragged along by my parents to church. While at school, I attended church out of fear of punishment. Later I went to church as an auto habit as I had been trained like that for a number of years. I never knew how to pray! At some point, after leaving the catholic school, I tended to stray away from the church especially when I was an undergraduate. Fortunately, I didn't stray too long. The good Shepherd saw to it that I was brought back on track. All of a sudden I developed an interest in church going and a fear for God – a fear out of respect for the creator!

Although God gave humans freewill, the fact is that sometimes they tend to behave as if they are dim-witted. Hence there is a need for God to constantly supervise and guide them.

MEDITATION

- God is committed to us as a father to his children. It means keeping ourselves open to the promptings that HE sends to us.

- God also can reveal himself to us but we have to be "childlike" and ask him to show us.

- To be childlike is to acknowledge that we were created to have an ongoing relationship with God – a relationship of love, trust and dependence.

- A shepherd keeps a continual WATCH over his flock—so that they are not stolen or consumed by the wolf. Just so, Christ watches over His flock by His awareness, so that no hurt comes to His elect, so that they are not mortally infected by sin, or ensnared by temptation. Christ has His shepherd's eyes to watch His flock, and He has His shepherd's staff to beat off the wolf.

Conversing with God:

Dear Lord, You are the Good Shepherd. Without you by my side I tend to go astray. You are so kind to lead me, guide me and protect me whenever I seek your help. I thank you for staying close to me to advise me when I am confused. I thank you for caring for me especially when I stray. Although I know your voice, sometimes I find it hard to comprehend what you say. Please help me to understand your voice clearly and to know what you need me to do whenever I encounter difficult situations.

2

HEAR THE WORD OF GOD

"I communicate to you through the scriptures/Bible"

Our Heavenly Father has established a personal line of communication with His children through the Holy Spirit for the immortality and eternal life of His children.

In the Bible, the mission of the Holy Spirit is described as testifying of the Father and the Son to guide us into truth and to show us all things we should do.

The personal line of communication through His Holy Spirit is the source of our testimony of truth, of our knowledge, and of our personal guidance from a loving Heavenly Father.

Every one of us has Holy Spirit within us for the personal line of communication with our Heavenly Father but we need to allow Him to connect with us by a willing spirit within us.

When I was at school I have heard the following many times but they actually made sense only when I got past my teenage years. It was only then God helped me to activate the Holy Spirit.

- There are those who hear the word but the devil comes and takes away the word.

- There are those who hear the word for some time and in time of testing fall away.

- There are those who hear the word but as they go on their way they are choked by the cares and riches and pleasures of life.

- There are those who, hear the word, hold it strong in an honest and good heart, and bear fruit with patience.

We have to listen and comprehend what is being taught, have complete trust in what God says and get transformed. This is the only way we can bring about spiritual health in our lives. We need to hear God's words as often as we can.

MEDITATION

- Jesus gave the Holy Spirit as a "compensation" for His absence, to perform the functions toward us which He would have done if He had remained personally with us. The Holy Spirit's presence within us enables us to understand and interpret God's Word. He leads in the way we should go in all spiritual things. He is the ultimate guide, going before, leading the way, removing obstructions, opening the understanding, and making all things plain and clear.

- The Holy Spirit has been sent to help us do the will of God and to strengthen us and counsel us. But He won't do anything until He is asked. It is prayer that puts His power within us to work. He's just waiting on us to call on Him – to hear from Him

If Faith cometh
by hearing the
Word of God...
Romans 10:17

Conversing with God

Our Heavenly Father!

Please help me to hear and understand every word of yours and make it to take root in my life. Let your word guide me in tackling the cares of the world in the manner you desire and help defeat the wickedness of the devil.

With you I can do anything.

I thank you for the gift of the Holy Spirit. I am confident that with His help I will be able to understand your Word and put it into action. Be my friend and prepare my heart to read your word and listen to what you have to say. Let the Holy Spirit inspire me to read the passages in the scriptures that will enable me to lead a pious life.

Lord, you and only you can help me. Shed light on things which hitherto I have failed to understand. Be my comforter when misfortune strikes me and I get into a state of despair. Also please help me to joyfully recount the numerous blessings you have bestowed on me and help me to share them with others.

When the worries and cares of the world make me go off track help me to regain my balance by reminding me of your word and live my life the way you want me to live.

3

JESUS THE LIFE GIVER

"The seven 'I am' Statements"

Jesus the son of God, was sent by God the Father to live among the sinners of the world to show how to live a life acceptable to God. He was of course concerned about the spiritual lives of His children.

Jesus made seven "I AM" statements, recorded in the Gospel according to John and it was clearly understood what He was declaring. He meant that He was the eternal God incarnate, the life giver.

1. Jesus said that "I am the Way, the Truth, and the Life" and went further to say "No one comes to the Father except through me."

    When Jesus said to the apostles "I am the way" he meant that the only path for our salvation is through him.

    By the words "I am the Truth" he said authoritatively that he came to fulfil the law of God and reveal God's will for people.

    In the words "I am the life" he spoke of his authority over our life and death.

2. Jesus said that "I am the bread of life". Bread was such a basic food item in Jesus' time that it becomes

synonymous for food in general. Jesus provides the spiritual food.

3. When Jesus said that "I am the light of the world" He was claiming that He is the exclusive source of spiritual light. Anyone who follows him shall not walk in darkness.

4. In saying that "I am the door" Jesus meant that As the Door, He is the one and only way of entrance into salvation.

5. As the Good Shepherd He is the one who cares for the sheep and provides for their salvation at the cost of His life. He lays down His life for the sheep.

6. When Jesus said that "I am the resurrection and life" He meant that resurrection on the last day shall be only "by Him" and therefore He could raise "now" as well." The "intention" of this saying seems to have been for the purpose of awakening faith in Martha that He could raise her brother Lazarus from the dead.

7. When saying "I am the Vine and the Father is the gardener" Every branch in Him that does not bear fruit, He takes away; and every branch that bears fruit, He prunes it so that it may bear more fruit.

I would have heard these words several times during various sermons at the churches I attended. They did not mean anything to me at that time. I realised later that some scripture verses only make sense when the Holy Spirit starts working within us. In his time only he activates us!

MEDITATION

- I was lost. Jesus showed me the way.

- I was surrounded by lies. Jesus showed me the truth.

- I thought I was living, but it wasn't until after I accepted Jesus that I had a life.

- Jesus brings the energy of light into our dark world.

- Jesus cares for us just like we need it.

- When life is hurting and chaos is all around, I commit to trust in Jesus. Trust means I place my life in the hands of the Lord. I do not let my heart to be troubled. I follow His direction in life even when things are going badly, going in a chaotic direction.

God has directly spoken and also spoken through the prophets. All are considered to be the word of God.

Conversing with God:

Lord Jesus, you are the way, the only way to God the Father in heaven. Thank you for being the way for me to be reconciled to him. I know that I can easily forget this at times. Please help me to remember this every day and to live with you at the centre of my life!

You are the Truth. I can so often be clouded by what others tell me is truth. Please help me to always know that you are the Truth. When I doubt please help me to be firm in your teachings. You are the Truth incarnate. Thank you for giving me the means of knowing the Truth, of living the Truth and of sharing the Truth. Please help me to share Your Truth with the rest of the world.

Jesus you are the Life. You know what is, what was and what is to come. I need not be afraid of death because in you I find life. You are life and I am thankful for eternal life with you and the Father. You have conquered death and brought me new life. Thank you for continuing to guide my life.

4

GOD'S PLAN FOR EACH ONE

"By my grace you are what you are"

God has a plan for each one's life, that means He has selected our destiny, and at decision points in our life our choices have been constrained in such a way as to give the result God chose but He allows us to have free will to choose the path to it.

Sadly, many reject eternal life which is the gift of God. That means they refuse His presence in their lives and thereby in reality do not have true life as God intended them to have. Those who decline God's grace are physically alive, but spiritually dead.

Human wisdom is foolish and inadequate to know God; our own thoughts are contrary to God's ways; our own desires are contrary to the Spirit of God.

We need to understand the difference between man's plan and God's plan in our search for a contented, joyful, full, and peaceful way of life.

The primary difference is that man's plan is oriented to self: to please self, to comfort self, to rely on self, to fulfill self, to forgive self, to exalt self, and to love self. This is described in Scripture as the old self-nature.

God's plan is to regenerate and change you. No person has within themselves the power to save or spiritually change themselves or establish a true relationship with God. It is God who does the changing as we in faith obey Him taking Him at His word. The more we submit to God as revealed in Scriptures, the more perfectly we will fit into his holy plan for our lives.

Throughout our adult life we connect with many people, some of whom we know well and others whom we meet in passing. Some of these people know the truth about God and his plan for each one of us and his love for the world. There are those who have misconceptions, some are far from God while others do not believe in the existence of God.

During my working life I have found myself in situations where I was surrounded by very sophisticated and educated people. I felt very inadequate when I tried to compare myself to them.

It took me a long time to realise the purpose of my life on earth. I finally realised that God had a plan for me and this plan was different to what God had for others. Comparing my life with others only tended to keep me away from God. God sees me differently to how I see myself.

God took me around the world exposing me to sophisticated people, some of whom ridiculed me while others acknowledged me for the good I was doing. By the grace of God I am what I am, I concluded.

MEDITATION

- God has a plan for your life. The Devil also has a plan for your life. Be ready for both. Just be wise enough to know which one to battle and which one to embrace! Pray to see God in your heart to light your way in your life.

- God's plan for your life is a lot better than the one you've been working on. If you decide to alter or abandon God's plan of salvation in Jesus Christ, then God's will cannot save that person, no matter how sincere they may be.

- Whenever you don't understand what is happening in your life, just close your eyes, take a deep breath and say to yourself " God I know it's your plan, just help me through it ....."

- This life is our preparation for living eternally in Heaven. So don't miss out on God's plan for you because you want to please other people or be successful in the eyes of the world.

- We may make plans for ourselves, but if God has something different in mind, He wins.

- God has given us free will and hence He allows us to make our mistakes but in time he brings us back on track.

- When our plans don't work and we get into a state of despair, we could ask God for guidance.

- We can consider ourselves blessed if our plans agree with God's plans.

- We must seek to know Him and not just seek to know about Him.

- God has created each of us to fulfil a specific role in this world. God can reveal this if we live in Him.

- God promises to give us the desires of our hearts, when our hearts are in line with His will and purpose.

Conversing with God:

Lord God you know every detail of my life, the number of hairs on my head, what brings me joy and what brings me sadness. By your grace you have made me into the person I am today.

You have given me so many opportunities and experiences that I am forever grateful. Through them, you have allowed me to come closer to you and to learn from you. Even when I make mistakes you still bring me back onto the right path and lead me to where you have called me. I believe that you know what is best for me, and I thank you for never giving up on me.

Please help me to continue to fulfil the plan you have for my life.

I am nothing without you. Thank you for loving me and for the love you have for the whole world. You have plans for each of us. Please help me to not compare what you have given to others with what you have given to me. Please help me to be happy with what you have given me and guide me to help others fulfil the task you have set for them.

By your grace I am what I am.

5

JESUS THE FRIEND IN NEED

"I shall look with favour and do wonderful things for you"

God causes all things to work together for the good of those who love and trust Him.

God's Word is filled with powerful exhortations to not be afraid.

When we are down and troubled and nothing is going right, and we need a helping hand close the eyes and think of Our Lord and just call out His name, and He'll always be there; He'll come running to help again and again. Winter, spring summer or autumn, all you have to do is call, and He'll be there... We have got a friend!

I often recall a particular incident in my life when I felt God was standing by my side and helping me out of distress.

It was in Zambia in 1980. I was returning from a town called Kabwe to Lusaka, 100 Km away with my young wife and three kids. All of a sudden my car fell into the pot holes on the road and my car's oil sump was sheared. Because all the oil ran out, my car engine seized. It was dark and I was in a land full of robbers and thugs.

I just closed my eyes and said "God, you are my only help, I trust you to get me out of this difficult situation."

I told my family to stay away from the roadside while I tried to stop someone to give me help. A number of cars and trucks passed by but no one wanted to stop. It is understandable that anyone would be scared to stop in a scary place like that.

Luckily one car stopped and there was this countryman of mine who couldn't do much except to say that he will go and inform someone known to me in Lusaka about my plight.

With hope, I continued to wave my hand and another car stopped for me. A gentleman, an African, got down from the car and asked me what the problem was. I told him what had happened and he said that the only help he can offer is to lend his towing chain which was in his car. I sighed with relief as then only it struck me that with a towing chain I can I ask someone to tow my car. The gentleman said he was the manager of the Lusaka Central bank and he couldn't believe when I said that I work in the building next to his office. He left after wishing me luck and requesting me to return the towing chain when it was convenient.

I was praying for some vehicle to stop and within the next ten minutes a trailer pulled to the side of the road. The first question the driver asked me was whether I had a towing chain. When I proudly said "yes", he jumped out of the truck, got the chain from me and did what was required to tow my car. I never had my car towed before and so I was very nervous especially with my family in the rear seat. God gave me the courage and strength to steer my car without causing any accident.

I thanked God for the timely help, first sending someone with a towing chain and then a trailer to take me and my family home safely. .

MEDITATION

- Hard times, bad times, tough times, I still have faith in God. Thank You Lord.

- Do Not Panic -- Trusting God in hard times requires refusing to be frightened, refusing to be immobilised, refusing to panic. No Matter What the Circumstances are, God Can Do It.

- Fear is the believer's greatest enemy. When a believer has fear, he cannot have faith. Fear paralyses, frustrates and cripples. Fear torments us.

- "Be strong, do not fear! Behold, your God will come with vengeance, with the recompense of God; He will come and save you. For I, the Lord your God, will hold your right hand, saying to you, 'Fear not, I will help you.'" (Isaiah 35:4; 41:13)

- Jesus is our friend, He cares for us. So we must yearn to ask for His help.

- Jesus will help us if we ask for his help and trust Him

- We don't have to be afraid and we don't have to feel alone because Jesus is always there.

Jesus the friend in need

Conversing with God:

Dear God, You are a mighty God who does great things in us. You go before us, you set the path and you guide and lead us. Thank you for directing my life when I am desperate. I know you work all things for good. Even in my darkest hour when I am full of despair I know I can count on you and put my trust in you. Time after time you have been there for me, pulling me forward.

I ask you to be with me when I start to doubt and tumble and fall. Please bring to my mind all the times that you have provided for me in the past and showered me with your love.

I am weak but you are strong. You carry me when I cannot walk anymore. Praise be to you always. I thank you for my past experiences that have shaped me into the person I am today.

Even if I don't always see it or understand I thank you for your timing. You know exactly what it is I require and when. You are never far from me; you are always by my side. Please help me to always fully rely and trust in you. Without you I can do nothing.

6

JESUS THE GIVER OF STRENGTH

"Come to me, all who labour and are heavy laden, and I will give you rest"

We all go through hard times in our lives. We lose our job, we fall sick, we have to deal with sickly loved ones and death in the family, we have misunderstanding with those whom we love and we meet with accidents and so on. Just like Jesus got his strength to go through His time of trials, we also somehow get the strength to go through hard times.

When we begin to trust God in our times of need, we will soon discover that there is divine strength available to us. It expresses itself intellectually, morally, physically, and spiritually, and arises at the moment it is needed to allow us to face and overcome our obstacles. This is the strength that the apostle Paul experienced over and over again. It is the power that is available to every child of God but only through total reliance upon Him.

The tragedies of our lives can be transformed into triumphs through the source of this strength—the person of Jesus Christ. When we, by faith, received Jesus Christ as our personal Lord and Saviour, He came to dwell within us in the presence of the Holy Spirit.

Essentially, all the strength to survive, the power to endure, and the ability to overcome are already abiding in us in the very presence of Jesus Christ through the Holy Spirit. Therefore, God doesn't have to send something down from heaven to enable us to face our trials. His greatest gift is already in our possession. Your responsibility is to trust Him, listen to Him, and live in obedience to Him.

It is much easier to handle hard times if we live with God.

We can all testify to the fact that more often than not some good comes out of the hard times we go through.

It was June 2004. My wife was diagnosed as having Leukaemia. She had to be in hospital and go through chemotherapy on a continuing basis for 20 months till she passed away in February 2006. Everyone including the doctor who treated my wife knew that there was no real cure for this deadly disease at that time. The doctor tried to prolong her life. I do not know where I got the strength but I was able to cope with 20 months of anguish and uncertainty. I felt that God was with me all the time giving the strength I needed. He made the whole episode look like a dream to me.

MEDITATION

- The problems and trials in our lives, help us to develop endurance.

- God's love lays an unshakable foundation for us to remain hopeful and patient in every trial and tribulation that comes our way.

- Our loving father who brings us trials will give us the strength to cope with them if we pray earnestly.

- As children of God, we can pray with confidence, always believing God will answer our prayers.

- Ask and it will be given to you; seek and you will find; knock and the door will be opened.

- God alone knows the perfect actions we should take and the right time to do so.

Conversing with God

Dear Jesus, when I am weak you are strong. You are my constant Lord Jesus when I as a human being tend to sway.

Jesus, you know when I sit down and when I rise. You know the struggles that I have been through and the struggles that I will face. You stand by me no matter what, and are always there to get me through even when I feel like giving up. Thank you for giving me the strength to push on and persevere.

Time and time again when things go wrong you turn even the hardest of times into something good. You help me to learn and show me the correct way to handle things. Thank you for being there for me always. I can do all things through you God who gives me strength. Please help me to be a witness to others of the mighty works and deeds you have done in my life, so through me others might come to know and rely on you. Your strength and power is far beyond my understanding, but without you I would not be able to cope. Thank you for always staying by my side. I know without you I can do nothing.

7

JESUS THE FORGIVER

"Forgive others as you have been forgiven by My Blood"

If we forgive others their trespasses our Heavenly Father will also forgive us. But if we do not forgive others their trespasses neither will our Father forgive our trespasses.

We're only human, we're all selfish, we all commit sins and make mistakes– whether or not we want to admit to them is another thing entirely! However, we may think that most of our "sins and mistakes" don't harm others while on the other hand when someone is abused we see things differently.

When it comes to forgiveness, many of us bring troubles and difficulties upon ourselves by an unforgiving attitude. We hold on to our hurts, our resentments and our anger rather than forgiving the one who has done us wrong. Holding on to all those negative emotions only hurts us in the long run – instead of the person who committed the wrongdoing!

A person with an unforgiving attitude can hardly be called a follower of Jesus Christ. Even of those who were so wicked they crucified their Saviour, He said: "Father, forgive them; for they know not what they do". When Peter asked the Lord how often he should forgive a person who sinned against him, "Till seven times?" Jesus answered, "I say not unto thee, until seven times: but, until seventy times seven times." It is wicked to reject a child of God simply because he made an error. We must be willing to forgive others.

People can and do change, and our duty is to forgive them. Some choose to learn from their sins and mistakes.

As we struggle towards that perfection which Jesus Christ holds out for us, let us give emphasis to forgiveness. Let us cultivate that aspect of our character and rejoice in the spirit of forgiveness, which is the comforting message of the atonement.

A trivial incident happened between my class mate and myself when we were in primary school. We refused to talk to each other following the misunderstanding. We completed primary schooling and moved to the same secondary school where we continued our enmity for each other. Other class mates sensing that we were enemies would arrange fights between us and enjoy the spectacle. When we were teenagers we belonged to the same cricket club where we had to work together. We did this well without talking to each other! Years went by, we left school and went our separate ways to do higher studies. After graduating, we both got married, I roamed the world and settled in Australia and my class mate did the same and finally settled down in the United States.

After nearly fifty years I realised how silly we had been. I sent an email to him and asked him why we were continuing our school day enmity and requested him to forgive me if I had offended him and forget all what happened when we were young and that we should be friends from now on. He replied immediately and expressed his true feelings and the desire to be my friend. Shortly after that, he visited Australia with his wife and made sure that we met. We had a wonderful few days together discussing all what happened in our lives in the lost fifty years. We now correspond to each other by email.

MEDITATION

- If we choose to live out the love of God, then forgiving is an option that cannot be avoided.

- Forgiving others releases us from anger and allows us to receive the healing we need.

- To forgive means to not seek revenge on the one who has hurt you.

- All people commit sins and make mistakes. God forgives them, and people are acting in a godlike (divine) way when they forgive. Forgiveness refers to the actor not the act.

- Forgiveness is a gift you give to yourself. It won't change your past, but it will change your future. It liberates you from the trap of endless revenge so that you can experience more joy and connection.

- The process of forgiving begins with a decision. You must understand that you've been locked up in the house of tortured bitterness long enough. Now it's time to leave for good. As we begin our journey, we can know that the Lord walks with us through this process.

- You have done what the Lord requires. You have done everything you could to make peace. The rest is in the Lord's hands.

Conversing with God

Dear Jesus, I thank you for forgiving my sins by dying for me on the cross. You have paid my debt and I am forever thankful for the new life you have bought for me. By your blood you have set me free from sin and death. Lord Jesus, please help me to forgive others as you have forgiven me.

I may have made a lot of mistakes in the past, through my actions, in what I have done and what I have failed to do. Through all of this you always show me mercy. Please help me to be merciful to others who may sin against me or cause me anguish. I know I am not perfect. No one in this world is perfect apart from you. Please give me the ability to always do what is right. Please develop in me a forgiving heart.

Lord God, if there is anyone in my life I have sinned against please help me to see the error of my ways and to seek forgiveness. Please give me an open heart to accept anyone should they come to me asking for forgiveness. Please help me to forgive them as you have forgiven me and help me to live a life pleasing to you.

8

A GOOD MARRIAGE PARTNER, GOD'S GIFT

Wives, be subject to your husbands, as is fitting in the Lord. Husbands, love your wives and do not be embittered against them (Colossians 3:18-19).

The key is for each wife to follow God's plan, know her part, and work to fit in with her husband's responsibilities.

I used to wonder for a long time what sort of girl was destined for me. Will she have the attributes I was after? All good things come from God. A good marriage partner is one of the greatest blessings that one can receive in this life. A good partner is a divine gift. The husband and wife are brought together by the providence of God. God will strengthen their relationship.

Not everyone is lucky to have a partner of noble character, ever loving and faithful.

It was the custom in the town I lived that parents find a suitable girl for the son – the so called proposed marriage. I had fallen in love with a girl who was related to me, who lived very close by and whom I thought was ideal for me. I admired this girl for a long time but through fear of upsetting my parents I kept my love to myself. When the time came for marriage my father having sensed that I had a soft corner for this girl made sure that he proposed that girl to me. God has been kind to me and everything worked in my favour though I was not the best qualified for her. Somehow I was selected from the various proposals and that was the best thing that happened to me in my life. I got married to her and within a short period we set out to live in England and later in several other countries. This kept me out of the local politics and interference from our parents and relatives. She gave me 42 wonderful years of life and three great boys.

MEDITATION

- Modern marriage is bound to be peaceful if there is mutual respect between the husband and wife.

- Communicating our needs requires and creates a great deal of respect and authenticity in our relationships. When you're honouring one another's needs, you're creating the opportunity for greater authenticity, respect, accountability, and love.

- A great relationship is about two things: first, appreciating the similarities, and second, respecting the differences.

- A couple that prays together, stays together.

- When a wife strives to model Christ, she influences her husband with her Godly behaviour.

- Successful marriage is based on God's principles. Man loves his wife. Woman submits to her husband.

- When a man has a good wife it is easily seen in his face.

- A young man is to seek the Lord's guidance in finding a mate as God's choice is much better — when submitting his will, desire and choice totally to God.

Conversing with God

Dear Lord, not every man is fortunate enough to meet and marry a woman of noble character in his life with characteristics described in the scriptures. I thank you for giving me a wonderful wife. Please help me to appreciate the worth of all virtuous women like my wife. Help them with the call you have placed on their lives. Help them to do your will all their lives. Clothed with strength and dignity enable them to help their husbands to be better men. They are worth far more than gold and so please bless them and make them do your will to the best of their abilities.

9

GOD IS OUR REFUGE AND STRENGTH

"I have the strength for everything through him who empowers me"

Life as we know does not always turn out as we plan it. Life is a battle field. Life is full of difficulties and obstacles from birth to death. This is a great truth.

God is our refuge and strength, a very present help in trouble. We must believe in Him, depend on Him, hide in Him, be still before Him and acknowledge His sovereignty in our life and circumstances. Once we truly understand and accept Our Lord, then difficulties in our life no longer matters.

The Lord helps his people to bear the difficulties they encounter, and he helps them out of their difficulties in the most proper and seasonable time. He sends difficulties to strengthen his people and to remind them of his presence.

I have had many experiences where God came to help me when I was in trouble. I believe that God helps if we have complete trust in him and ask him for a specific help. He renders help using other people.

A classic example of a help I used to get was when I was an applied mathematics teacher in high schools around the world. I was in the habit of giving difficult tasks to students some of which I myself would have found it difficult to solve. Yet I would boldly attempt the question on the black/white board knowing with certainty that I would get stuck at some point. But I was confident that God will step in and guide me. To my amazement someone in the class would come out with some idea which I had not thought of. Using that idea I would proceed and complete the answer to the problem. This is just one of those simple instances where you feel that God is an ever present help in trouble.

MEDITATION

- When I put my trust in you O Lord, you give me strength.

- When you hold my hand in my weakness I rise above the challenges in my life.

- God, you are so merciful to assign angels to keep watch on each of us.

- Your angels Lord, are at work in our lives, protecting us and guiding us.

- Your angels Lord, protect us from harm either by rescuing us from danger or preventing us from entering a dangerous situation.

Conversing with God

Dear Lord

Thank you for always being present in my life, even when I may not always acknowledge you. I know that with you I can overcome all difficulties and obstacles that come my way. You give me strength to continue moving forward when I feel like giving up. Your timing makes all things work out for good. I may not always understand the plans you have and the way things work out but I trust that you have my life in your hands.

Please help me to come to you with trust and expectant faith when I face troubles. I know that you have never let me down and will always lead me out of difficulties back onto the right path. I thank you for putting people in my life and using them to help me. Your timing may not always make sense to me but over and over you prove that you are greater than the timelines I put on you. You are my refuge, especially when times are tough. You give me strength to continue going when all I want to do is stop. Thank you for always providing a way for me, without you I can do nothing.

10

BIBLE CONDEMNS ASTROLOGY

"All the needs of the Christian believer are met through God and His word"

Faithful Christians always oppose astrology on the basis of intellectual and scriptural foundation. For curiosity and amusement, millions of ordinary citizens read the daily horoscopes published in mass-circulation newspapers. Some get their horoscopes done by astrologers and also get guided by their forecasts.

However, the Bible strongly denounces astrology, divination, witchcraft, and other occult practices. The strict stance taken by the Bible is due to the fact that people are trying to get answers about life's questions from a source other than God.

I was introduced to astrology when I was about 18 years by my father who had been brought up in a Hindu environment. Astrology is part and partial of the Hindu Religion. I just couldn't understand the astrological jargon then. Later in my life, as a mathematician I was curious to know what astrology is all about and read a few books. I realised that it was a pseudo-science and somehow some of the things astrologers foretell do turn out correct. I used to think that some astrologers were cheating people and trying to make money. So I put some astrologers to the test. I would consult two or three astrologers to see whether everyone is saying the same thing about the point at issue. Sometimes they all say the same thing and other times there would be differences of opinion. It came to light that error in calculations could be the reason for this. I tended to believe that astrology provided a similar sort of guidance to the weather forecast. One may even liken consulting an astrologer to consulting a psychologist. A good astrologer may be considered as providing mental relief to those in distress. Having said that I assert that good Christians should trust God and his words and disregard astrology. This way they would conform to the Bible and the law of the Church.

We don't need to know the future when we trust in God. Our future is in his hands. His hands are safe hands.

There is great danger in being told the future. It can create great fear which can destroy the present enjoyment of life. Also there is the risk of "self fulfilling" prophecy whereby because we believe something will happen, we cause it to happen by our own actions based on the belief we have. If we think we will fail then most likely we will

MEDITATION

- Astrology evolved from the crude, superstitious worship of the planets.

- Astrology is the "interpretation" of an assumed influence the stars and planets exert on human destiny.

- God alone knows our future. There is no astrologer who can predict our life's events with absolute certainty.

- If there is a need to understand perplexing situations in our lives, we should turn to God in prayer.

- any 'knowledge' gained through the practice of Astrology is demonic in nature, not 'Heavenly':

Bible condemns astrology

Conversing with God

God, help me to continually keep my faith in you and to turn away from wrong beliefs. You meet all my needs God, through your son Jesus Christ and your word. Holy Spirit, please guide me to do your will and lead me in the right path.

Please stop me from straying far from you and the good plans you have for me. With your help I can turn away from my wrong beliefs and live a life worthy of your calling. When I have doubts please draw me to your word and lead me to the passage you have chosen specifically for me. In times of distress please send me relief and comfort. Enable me to understand the love you have for me, and help me to only put my trust in you. You have great plans for me, I don't need to try and predict my future. In you I can trust that whatever it is, it will be for my good and not for harm.

11

GOSSIPERS AND BULLIES, A NUISANCE

"Love your enemies and pray for those who persecute you"

Love your enemies, bless those who curse you, do good to those who hate you, and pray for those who spitefully use you and persecute you.

Gossip is idle talk or rumour about someone and is almost always done behind the back of the subject of the gossip.

People gossip in order to hurt those whose popularity, talents, or lifestyle they envy.

The Bible tells us to keep our mouths shut unless it is necessary and appropriate to speak. Gossipers stir up trouble and cause anger and bitterness and pain among people.

I felt very uncomfortable during my entire working life as a teacher when I had to live among gossipers and bullies. I had to make conscious effort to avoid contacts with such people to guard against hurtful comments.

People gossip for various reasons. It may be that they want to feel superior or they are bored or they envy the other person's popularity and success or they want to attract attention.

People who bully others feel weak, inferior and inadequate.

I realised that colleagues at work place gossiped about me and bullied me because I was a popular teacher who was held in high esteem by the students and the bosses wherever I taught. I was blessed as God gave me the strength to destroy their efforts.

MEDITATION

- if someone is gossiping because of jealousy, just keep sending them more good news about you.

- When surrounded by bullies, build some support around you!

Conversing with God

Dear Lord,

Thank you for always loving me and being with me. Please give me the strength to love my enemies and to each day pray for those who persecute me.

Your example shows me the way you want me to live. So many hated you and cursed you yet you died for all of their sins. What I encounter cannot compare to what you endured. Please help me to always bless and not curse those who spitefully use me and persecute me. It is so different to what the world tells me to do, but with your help I can show the world the way you have called us all to live.

Please give me the gift of discernment, especially when it comes to when you require me to speak and when to remain quiet. At times I tend to be too quiet and let gossipers to cause pain. Please help me to give life and goodness to those I meet. Comfort me when others gossip about me or bully me and give me the strength to continue in the path you have called me to.

12

HUMILITY BEGETS HONOUR

"Humble yourselves before the Lord, and he will lift you up"

Humility is the quality of being humble. It is opposite of definition of ego, self-sufficiency, boastfulness, arrogance, pride and aggressiveness.

Humility is simply not thinking of yourself. Amongst the benefits described in the Bible are honour, wisdom, eternal life, unity, rewards in heaven and others.

Humility opens us to the world. Humility before God is nothing if not proved in humility before fellow humans..

It is easy to think we humble ourselves before God: humility towards others will be the only sufficient proof that our humility before God is real.

If we meet our bosses or other superiors and feel nervous and in awe for them, then we are experiencing humility.

The bible says, humble yourselves under the mighty hand of God so that at the proper time he may exalt you.

It was in 1977, after 18 years as a teacher in various countries that I qualified in accounting and worked as an accountant in Zambia. I got a lucky break after much struggle to work as an accountant. No one would consider me for an accountant post as I did not have any practical experience. I needed to start somewhere and I prayed continually and God finally fulfilled my cry.

The manager of the company in which I was to work somehow came to know of me through an application I had sent to his organisation years ago. I was invited for an interview from Malawi where I was lecturing in accounting. This to me, was a definite divine help.

He offered me the position of Management Accountant at a certain salary. I was honest and told him that I may need some help during the first few months. He assured me of his help and I was happily working. One of my duties was preparing the payroll for the company each fortnight.

The managing director of the holding company was at logger head with my manager. They hated each other. He was mad that my manager had appointed a man with no experience. Anyway, within a short period there was a restructure under the big boss's guidance and everyone's salary was increased significantly and I was not given any increase. I was very willing to work for the same salary and I minded my duties without grumbling. After two years, my manager got another lucrative job and was going to leave me. To my surprise, a few days before he left, he called me to his office with the Human Resources Manager, gave a talk on my excellent performance during his tenure and in front of me signed the necessary Personnel Action Form, raising my salary to approximately to twice the amount. It so happened that this amount was even more than the chief accountant's salary!

I thanked God profoundly for rewarding me for my humility.

MEDITATION

- We can resolve arguments when we are humble

- We can handle unfair treatment peacefully when we are humble.

- We do not have to put on a "false front" when we are humble.

- When we are humble, we can respond to and learn from criticism without becoming defensive.

- We can ask for forgiveness when we are humble.

- We can <u>talk with the right attitude</u> **when we are humble.**

- To do always well and to consider oneself as nothing is the sign of a humble soul.

Humility begets honour

Conversing with God

Dear Lord,

Please help me to always walk humbly and to trust in you. I believe that you know what is best for me and in your timing you will make all things work together for good. Through your example I am able to be humble and allow you to lift me up to where you want me to be. I make my own plans but you direct my path. You know the desires of my heart and when I call out to you, you answer me. Please help me to grow in humility and to overcome my pride that so often can hold me back. Please help me to not become despondent when others try to rule over me, but help me to humble myself in front of them and trust that in your timing you will raise me to new heights. Thank you for rewarding me for my humility, and giving me the example of your son. Please help me to remain humble even when I am given good gifts or placed in a place of honour.

13

ANGER CAUSES TROUBLE

"But I tell you, anyone who says, 'You fool!' will be in danger of the fire of hell"

When we are angry, we are at the mercy of an unpredictable and powerful emotion accompanied by physiological and biological changes in our body. It leads to troubles, damages and losses. It causes separation.

When we speak with anger, we don't care how our listeners feel and try to respond. We make them defenseless as we expect that only our points of view are heard. So our listeners are unable to communicate with us. Our attitude creates frustration, confusion, confrontation, anger, bitterness, regret, separation, revenge, etc. for our listeners.

A fool gives full vent to his anger, but a wise man keeps himself under control.

A fool is a person who acts unwisely – a silly person. A synonym for fool is idiot! The term idiot actually refers to a person with intellectual disability.

I was very well-respected by both managers and colleagues in the company I worked for in Zambia. An incident happened and I had lost my temper and called a colleague of mine an idiot. I was in real trouble with the management.

It happened when I was to leave my family in Zambia and go to Yugoslavia on business for a week with my General Manager and another colleague.

There was a major repair to be done to the sewerage system in my house. I had requested the gentleman who was in charge of this repair work to attend to the matter before I left for Yugoslavia. I had reminded him a couple of times. Despite my reminders he ignored my request. The day before my flight I stormed into his office and yelled at him very angrily (very unlike me) calling him an idiot.

After my yelling the work was done but he had complained about me to the management and pleaded that they take severe action against me for calling him an idiot (a bad word to use in that country).

After I returned from Yugoslavia, a meeting of the disciplinary committee comprising of various managers was called and I was asked to explain my unruly behaviour. They asked me whether I understood the consequences of calling someone an idiot. They demanded that I apologise to the offended person.

After my explanation and apology I was warned not to repeat this behaviour. This being my first offence I escaped without any penalty.

MEDITATION

- Intelligent people think before they speak.

- A moment of patience in a moment of anger prevents a thousand moments of regret.

- A harsh word spoken at the time of anger is so much more poisonous.

- Respect the other person's feelings, and values, without judging or criticising

- Don't answer the foolish arguments of fools, or you will become as foolish as they are.

Conversing with God:

Dear Lord,

Please help me to always follow your example and steer me clear from the fire of hell.

I can't control what other people do Lord, but I can change the way I act and treat them. Please help me to always treat them with love and kindness and to see them as you see them, one of your children you created lovingly.

When I get annoyed help me to not lose my temper but instead to think of you and the way you treated everyone while you were on Earth.

Lord please help me to always repent and come to you with a humble and contrite heart. Help me to make amends to those I may injure through my thoughts, words and deeds. Thank you for always loving me and for sending your son Jesus Christ to forgive my sins and reconcile me to yourself.

Your mercy endures forever, help me to be merciful to others when they may wrong me. Please give me humility to seek mercy and forgiveness when I make mistakes. Thank you for the mercy that was shown to me. Please help me to learn from the error of my ways and lead me to path you have set out for me.

14

ALCOHOL HARMS THE BODY

"Wine is a mocker, strong drink a brawler, and whoever is addicted is not wise"

Anyone who reacts adversely to alcohol for any reason should not drink alcohol privately or socially at all.

The Bible contains examples and commands against excessive use of alcohol and drunkenness. (e.g. 1 Tim 5:23) Alcohol is habit forming. "We first make our habits, and then our habits make us.» - John Dryden.

Alcohol can be used wisely or be abused. Generally speaking using alcohol is harmful to the body. When used in moderation it does help some people to feel good. Blessed are those who never got used to this bad habit.

Drunkenness on the other hand is the state of being intoxicated by consumption of alcohol to a degree that mental and physical facilities are noticeably impaired and that can cause undesirable results.

I developed the habit of drinking at the age of 21 just after my graduation, when in the company of my friends. My parents did not know that I was drinking. The time had come for me to leave my parents and go overseas and one day my father gave me a lecture on drinking alcohol, maybe because he sensed that I was drinking with friends. He talked about getting addicted to alcohol and of the dangers of social drinking! He said that while overseas I will have the temptation to drink and I should then guard myself against excessive drinking.

For a few months he invited me to have a drink with him at home on Sunday nights. He introduced me to many different kinds of alcohol. I used this drug in moderation throughout my life and without it I would not have been able to achieve the things I did in life.

I am lucky and thank God for not letting me go astray. Anyone with no self-control and who tends to be boisterous after taking drinks would go astray and therefore should try to avoid this bad habit.

MEDITATION

- Alcohol is not a necessity of life.

- Alcohol's hidden harms usually only emerge after a number of years. And by then, serious health problems can have developed.

- The effects of alcohol on our health will depend on how much we drink. The more we drink, the greater the health risks.

- When we drink alcohol, it's absorbed into our bloodstream and affects every part of our body. In the long term, this can put our health at serious risk.

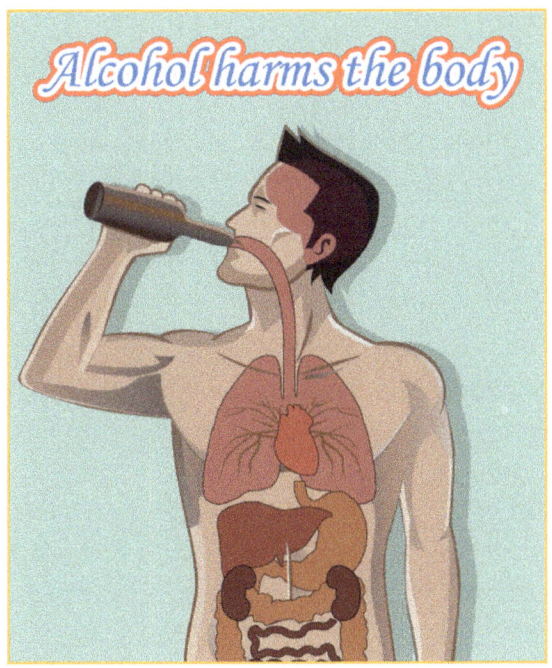

Conversing with God

Dear Lord,

Thank you for always guiding me and for helping me whenever I am in danger of being led astray. I thank you for giving me a strong will power to make my own choices.

Please help me to always have a clear mind and to not be inebriated by substances such as alcohol. I thank you for helping me not to abuse alcohol but use it in moderation. This has always helped me with all the writing I have been doing in my life.

Thank you for guiding me throughout my life and protecting me from situations that could have led me to my demise. Thank you for making me associate with the right people and to lead a respectable and responsible life.

15

A FRIEND IN NEED IS A FRIEND INDEED

"The greatest love you can show is to give your life for your friends"

The verse above implies that one must put their friends first and make their need more important than one's own. It is about being selfless and sacrificial in one's actions towards others rather than selfish.

There are some people in this world who will only be there for you as long as you have something they need. When you no longer serve a purpose to them, they will leave. Over time we weed these people out of our life and are left with a few good people we can count on. We are able to gradually figure out who our real friends are.

Good friends fight for you, respect you, include you, encourage you, need you, deserve you and stand by you.

I was a nomad and so I did not have many long lasting friends. There were a few short term friends and I never forget them.

A particular friend who comes to my mind is one I got to know in Malawi Polytechnic and after two years we both moved to Zambia.

At the time I was winding up my affairs in Zambia to migrate to Australia; I had sold my car and was using a car that the company I worked for gave me.

Unfortunately, one day some car thieves followed my car into my garage at home and at gun point took it away from me. I was therefore without a vehicle for about two weeks and none of my well known compatriots came to offer any help by way of transport. This friend, on hearing my plight, came over to my home and offered his car. He said that he doesn't use his car much and that I could use it till I left the country. He was really selfless and was sacrificial in his actions towards me. He is indeed a real friend.

MEDITATION

- Ask not what a friend can do for you. Ask what you can do for a friend.

- "Misfortune shows those who are not really friends."- Aristotle.

- A true friend is hard to find. If we want to create lasting friendships, we need to be trustworthy, caring, kind, supportive, honest and positive.

- True friends will tell us the truth even when it hurts.

- "Walk with the wise and become wise, for a companion of fools suffers harm." Choose Your Friends Carefully

- Sometimes everybody in our boat isn't rowing. Some are drilling holes when we're not looking. Know the circle".

- A good friendship requires two things - To find similarities and to respect differences. Friends do not always agree with one another because everyone has different interests, likes and dislikes. Therefore friends need to learn to compromise with one another.

• "The best way to destroy an enemy is to make him a friend, and the best way to make someone a friend is to give them that accolade in your mind". – Abraham Lincoln

Conversing with God

Dear Jesus,

Please help me to be a good friend by following your example. Create in me a heart to give and not to count the costs, to be selfless and sacrificial rather than put my own selfish desires above other people's needs. You showed us that the greatest love is to lay down one's life for their friends. Please help me to lay down my life for my friends daily.

Help me Lord to know who my real friends are, to discern and know in whom I should invest my time. Thank you for those people you have brought into my life, especially those that have been able to help me grow into the person I am today. Please bless the friends I am still close with and those whom you called me to be friends with for only a á limited time in my life.

I thank you for the gift of friendship and the friends that you have blessed me with in my life. I know that not everyone is lucky enough to have good friends. Please help me also to be a great friend.

DIVINE INTERVENTION IN THE LIVES OF MY ASSOCIATES

16

RELIEVED OF MENTAL AGONY

"For I the LORD your God will hold your right hand, saying to you, Fear not; I will help you."

Severe physical pain can cause intense feelings of suffering. Long-lasting physical pain can cause stress and a feeling of depression. Physical pain takes time to subside, and as the wound or illness that caused the pain heals, the pain will ease.

Mental pain is psychological. When bad things happen, it can take a while to get over the mental pain. Emotional and psychological trauma is the result of extraordinarily stressful events that shatter our sense of security, making us feel helpless and vulnerable.

The following story is that of Regina of Sydney Australia:

During the 72 years of my life to-date God has been very kind and merciful to me many times and surprised me.

At the age of 38 when I was a mother of two boys, I used to suffer from terrible stomach pain for a long time. I used to attribute it to gastric problems and was very negligent. Furthermore, I used to be mortally afraid of injections and operations. I imagined that it could be appendicitis and because of my fear of operations I was postponing my visit to the doctor. My sons somehow talked me into agreeing to see the doctor by giving me the courage and strength.

I went to the hospital thinking that the doctor was going to perform the operation for appendicitis which everyone said was a simple operation. The doctor found out that the pain I had was not because of appendicitis but was due to a growth in my stomach. He spoke to my husband and got his signature agreeing for the immediate removal of the growth.

The operation was successful and I learned after the operation that the doctor had not only removed the growth but also my ovary and that the doctor had to put in18 stitches.

My husband told me later that the growth was about the size of a small coconut and the operation was a major one.

If I had known this before the operation I would have died of fear. By God's grace everything went off well. I thank God profoundly even now for relieving me of the terrible agony I would have had to go through had I known the actual situation.

MEDITATION

- The power of our mind can decrease our physical pain.

- Any mind based technique can have control over mental pain.

- Mindfulness meditation can alleviate suffering associated with physical, psychosomatic and psychiatric disorders.

Conversing with God

Lord God, you are always there for us whenever we face struggles. You are our guide and protector; you know what is best for us. You pick us up when we fall down, and when we don't feel like standing up or moving forward, you hold us and help us.

Thank you for sending people into our lives who have been able to guide us and keep us safe. Thank you for the peace you give us, the peace that only you can give that is not of this world. Without it we would be in terrible agony and would not be able to press on.

Thank you for your loving kindness and the mercy that you continue to show us each and every day of our lives. Your grace is enough for us, please help us to truly know and appreciate all that you have done for us in our lives. Please help us to share with others your love. Help us not to fear but to share the hope we have in you. Please give us the courage to persevere when we feel like quitting. Without you, we can do nothing but with you we can do all things.

17

ADVERSITY TURNS OUT TO BE A BLESSING

"We rejoice in our sufferings, knowing that suffering produces endurance"

Suffering may come because God has a great plan in our future even when we are counted righteous in His eyes. The scriptures tell us Job was wealthy, happy, faithful to God, and had a great family. Then, he lost everything — children, property and wealth, good name and even his health. Why did God allow Job to suffer such tragedies? Because God challenged the devil with Job's obedience and faith. Even in the midst of great suffering, Job trusted God and uttered: "Though he slay me, I will hope in him."

Suffering may come for reasons that we don't understand unless or until God reveals them to us.

Our misfortunes in life can be used to strengthen our character and realise our goals, no matter how difficult. We have to bravely face hardship to enrich our life.

We don't develop courage by being happy every day. We develop it by surviving difficult times and challenging adversity.

The story below is also that of Regina of Sydney:

During the 25th July 1983 communal riots in Sri Lanka our house was burgled and we lost everything including money and jewelry. My husband was at his work place at that time but there he was miraculously saved from thugs. My husband and I with the two sons ended up in a camp where we stayed for two weeks. While in the camp I couldn't help curse God for putting us into such a situation. When I looked at the other families and learned of their pathetic stories I thanked God for sparing us without any bodily harm or death to any four of us.

Through this incident he showed us a new life by bringing us to Australia. Our migration to this developed country paved the way for first class education to our boys. We were also able to save much more than what we lost in Sri Lanka.

We got the two sons married at the appropriate time. The two gorgeous daughters in law gave us three grandchildren each. God has even blessed us with fifty years of married life and the children and grandchildren helped us celebrate the milestone anniversary. We sincerely thank God for his mercy on us and we will not cease to praise him for all the blessings he has showered on us.

MEDITATION

- In every adversity there lies the seed of an equivalent-advantage. In every defeat is a lesson showing how to win the victory next time. - Robert Collier

- Just when the caterpillar thought its life was over, it became a butterfly. Does a butterfly crawl back into its cocoon and become a caterpillar?

- Failure stories help us to have strength and new Ideas to win. From Success stories we have only the messages.

- Prayer is the best armour against all trials. God understands our prayers even when we can't find the words to say them.

Conversing with God

Dear Lord,

You are so good and know exactly what we need.

Lord Jesus, you know when we sit down and when we rise, you know everything about us. Thank you for leading and guiding us throughout our lives, from the day we were conceived until the day you call us home to you to eternal life in heaven.

Throughout our life you have made us to rejoice in suffering as suffering produces endurance. Please help me to remember this next time I go through trials you give and take away. Help me to know that nothing I could ever lose on earth compares with how much you have already won for me through your son Jesus' death on the cross. When I am weak, you are strong.

Help me to rely on you and lean on you rather than my own strength. Time and time again you show me your goodness and yet I sometimes forget. With your help I can do all things. You pour out your blessings on me and your mercy is like an endless waterfall cleansing me from all unrighteousness.

Lord God, please help me to be merciful as you are merciful to me, and to give to others like you have given to me.

18

SURVIVING DEATH IN RIOTS

"I call on the LORD in my distress, and he answers me"

When disasters become severe and things beyond human capacity happen unexpectedly, we can only call on God and say, "My refuge and my fortress, my God, in you I trust."

God is our refuge and strength, a very present help in trouble.

A riot is generally characterized by thugs lashing out in a violent public disturbance causing damage to property and endangering lives.

Sri Lanka has experienced ethnic tensions between its majority Sinhalese and minority Tamils and Moors populations for nearly hundred years.

The following story is related by Christine of Sydney.

Beginning in the capital Colombo, Sri Lanka on the night of 24 July 1983, the racial riots spread to other parts of the country. Over seven days Sinhalese mobs attacked Tamil targets, burning, looting and killing.

The July 1983 racial riots in Sri Lanka were the worst of all the riots. The Tamils in the Sinhalese areas were in great danger of losing their lives. At that time I was living with my family in Kalutara, a town approximately 66 Km away from Colombo.

Our oldest son was three years old and I was pregnant with the second child.

We heard the rumour that an employee in the organisation where my husband worked had organised a gang of thugs to kill my family. Our land-lord noticing one of the thugs standing in front of our house and watching us quickly alerted us and helped us to move to the house behind ours for safety. We were helpless but called on God and hoped He would do something.

My husband tried to contact his employer and he didn't care to come to our aid. Fortunately, a friend of my husband who was a security officer at his work place and living close by to us sensing the danger we were in called the police immediately. To our surprise the police came without delay and whisked us away to a refugee camp.

Everything happened so fast and our lives were saved miraculously. We are ever so thankful to God for his timely intervention.

In my distress I cried out to the LORD, and He answered me!

MEDITATION

- Whenever we face a problem beyond the human ability to solve it, God Is the only solution. Only God could help us. The only condition for receiving God's solution is faith.

- "Every saint has a past, and every sinner has a future." — Oscar Wilde

- God chooses the unqualified and makes them qualified.

Conversing with God

Loving father, we thank you for your timely protection in times of grave danger. Your faithfulness and mercy remain the same yesterday, today and forever. Even though the people we trust betray us you are ready to send someone we least expected to come to our rescue in times of need. You are true to your word that you are our shield and strength.

19

SUCCESSFUL KIDNEY
TRANSPLANT

"I am the Lord who heals you"

If God answers your prayer, He is increasing your faith. If He delays, He is increasing your patience. If He doesn't answer, He has something better for you.

"Do not be anxious about anything, but in everything, by prayer and petition, with thanksgiving, present your requests to God." -Philippians 4:6

A kidney transplant is an operation in which a person with kidney failure receives a new kidney.

The new kidney can come from living donors or from unrelated donors who have died. A living donor may be someone in the family such as the spouse. It may also be from a close friend. In some cases, it may be a stranger who wishes to donate a kidney to anyone in need of a transplant. There are advantages and disadvantages to both types of kidney transplants.

The following kidney transplant story is that of Mahadevan of Sydney.

My kidneys started malfunctioning in October 1989. I started to take medications from October 1992. The kidney function seemed somewhat stable till January 2002. Then my kidney specialist informed me that kidneys were starting to deteriorate and in September 2003 my kidneys stopped functioning completely. At that point I began dialysis three times a week for two years.

I had to leave my job in November 2004 because of my health. I had the option of considering a kidney transplant. However, this meant a probable long wait for the doctors to find a well-matched kidney for me. By God's grace my wife's blood group is the same as mine and she was quite willing to donate one of her kidneys to me. When the doctors compared our blood samples there was only one criterion match out of a possible six but my kidney specialist decided to go ahead with the transplant.

In September 2005, we had the kidney transplant surgery. After my surgery was over, the doctors were concerned because the arteries of the kidney did not function for twenty minutes. Then the arteries started functioning and the new kidney was working. I believe that was intervention by God.

It is almost ten years now since the kidney transplant and my kidney is functioning extremely well. I thank God for His grace and mercy.

MEDITATION

- "Sometimes it takes a painful experience to make us change our ways". When we put our cares in God's hands, He puts His peace in our Hearts.

- Do Your Part And God Will Do His. God is always faithful to his part if you do yours. Bu doing your part must come first. If you don't your part, don't blame God.

- I will take sickness away from the midst of you and the number of your days I will fulfill (Ex. 23:25, 26).

- God is the source of everything

- I have redeemed you from every sickness and every plague (Deut. 28:61 and Gal. 3:13).

- I am the health of your countenance and your God (Ps.43:5).

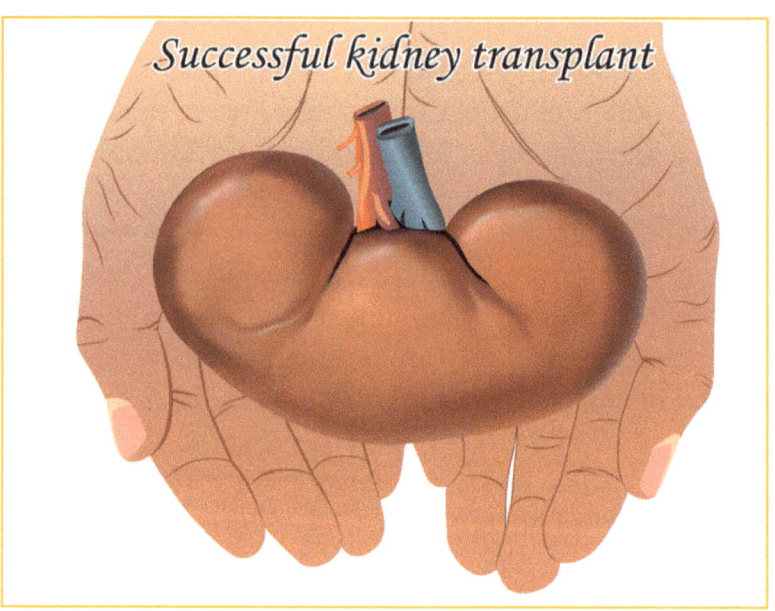

Successful kidney transplant

Conversing with God

Father God, I thank you for the blessings of medical science through which you work to help and preserve our lives. I pray for those who are unwell and especially for those who need transplant surgery that you would grant success to such surgery. Thank you for those who unselfishly donate body organs. I pray that you would continue to help those in the medical profession to continue to find new ways of bringing help and healing to people who are unwell. To you be all glory, honour and praise.

20

MUCH HELPFUL FINANCING

"My God will meet all our needs……"

The causes of financial difficulty can include sickness, natural disaster, unemployment or over commitment. Most people especially the migrants to a new country experience financial difficulty. Most countries do provide financial relief to these migrants at least at the start when they are settling in.

"People tend to think their circumstances determine the quality of their lives. So they pour their energy into trying to control those situations. They feel happy when things are going well, and sad or frustrated when things don't turn out as they had hoped. They rarely question the correlation between circumstances and feelings. Yet it is possible to be content in any and every situation. Put more energy into trusting God and don't let your well-being depend on circumstances." - Sarah Young

There are days when it's not easy trusting God.

Schedules are too full. Work is too hard. Pressures are too much. Money is too tight. Needs are too many. Loss is too great.

The Apostle Paul reminds us that God will meet or supply all of our needs - financial, emotional, relational, positional, social and physical "according to His glorious riches in Christ Jesus." Often, this kind of "trust" requires us to learn, love and lose.

Remember, prayer is conversation with God. "Ask and it will be given to you; seek and you will find; knock and the door will be opened to you. - Jesus

Be encouraged. He will supply . . . He will fill every empty bucket you have.

Mahadevan of Sydney has the following story on how his financial predicament was resolved.

In July 2011, I had a fall in the bath room and hit my neck on the wash basin and I was paralysed from neck downwards. I was admitted to Royal North Shore Hospital in Sydney for surgery and treatment. In October 2011 I was transferred to the Royal Rehabilitation Centre. There I went to the rehabilitation process and my discharge date was marked as 31 March 2012. Afterwards it was extended to 31 July 2012.

During this period of nine months our social worker was requesting home care assistance every month but it was rejected every time on the grounds that there were 500 people ahead of me in the waiting list. Then our doctor advised that we write to our local member of parliament. In the meantime we were asked to go to a nursing home which would have cost us $100 per day which was far beyond our income. However, by God's grace, our letter to the local member to the parliament was referred to the Minister of Age Care Services and we got the Home Care Service funded by the government in mid-September 2012.

We were able to return home in October 2012 after the formalities were completed. This saved us from severe financial difficulties. All glory to God.

MEDITATION

- Be grateful for all the obstacles in your life. They have strengthened you as you continue with your journey. "If God sends us on stony paths, he provides strong shoes."

- "The struggle of life is one of our greatest blessings. It makes us patient, sensitive, and Godlike. It teaches us that although the world is full of suffering, it is also full of the overcoming of it." - — Helen Keller

- "Trust in The Lord with all your heart. Don't lean on your own insights or answers. In all your situations, acknowledge His control and He will guide, direct and lead you."(Prov 3:5-6)

- "Never be afraid to trust an unknown future to a known God."

- God is our Provider. God does more. "Bow to Him who can do immeasurably more than all we ask or imagine, according to His power that is at work with us."

- I consider that our present sufferings are not worth comparing with the glory that will be revealed in us. And we know that for those who love God all things work together for good, for those who are called according to his purpose. (Romans 8: 18&28)

Conversing with God

Father God, we thank you for your timely intervention which saved us from severe financial difficulties. You have provided and protected us so far and you will continue to do so till the very end. All glory and praise be to you.

21

HEALING AT THE RETREAT CENTRE

"Do not fear, I am with you"

Divine healing is the work of God where people are healed physically, emotionally, mentally, and/or spiritually.

If we want to experience God's healing in our lives, we need to believe that God can heal us.

I will restore you to health and heal your wounds,' declares the LORD. - Jeremiah 30:17

"Faith sees the invisible, believes the unbelievable, and receives the impossible."

Is there any sick among you? Let him call for the elders of the church; and let them pray over him, anointing him with oil in the name of the Lord. - *James 5:14*

Who forgives all your iniquities; who heals all your diseases? - *Psalms 103:3*

When you open your mind to positive healing, the most amazing things can happen to you if you have Faith.

Philomena of Canberra experienced faith healing which she describes below:

I was born in Sri Lanka. I lived in France from 1980 to 1993 and migrated with my ailing husband to live with my daughters in Canberra, Australia. My husband passed away within a short period thereafter.

Since 1987 I had been having an acute pain in my right shoulder and arm joint. I had treatment both in France and in Australia but the pain continued to persist. I was having great difficulty in raising my right hand high and carrying my hand bag. This resulted in me using left hand for everything and my left shoulder also started to give a similar problem from February 2001.

In 1998, I had gone on a pilgrimage to India and I had the opportunity to visit the Divine Retreat Centre in Chalakudy, Kerala. This divine centre had a great appeal to me and in July 2001, I went there again, this time to take part in a retreat conducted in English. I went with the faith that my shoulder pain would be healed. The week's retreat started on Sunday and the participants left the centre by 2 PM on Friday after the Anointing Service.

On Tuesday morning, after the confession I went back to the church hall where Sr. Theresa was conducting a "Praise and Worship" session. Everyone was standing with their hands raised high up, singing and praising God. I couldn't raise my hands and I felt very sad. A few minutes later Sr. Theresa announced "Four people having difficulty raising their hands to praise the Lord are getting healed". Immediately I exclaimed and raised my hands - they went up with no pain! Both my shoulders were completely healed.

In 2002, a feeling of uneasiness developed in me which went for a long time. I used to have bad dreams and wake up in the nights with fear.

In July 2003 I went again to the Divine Centre for a week retreat. On the second day of the retreat I went for confession and counselling. I cleared my doubts and guilt feelings. I prayed to Lord Jesus to take away my bad dreams and fears.

During one of the adoration sessions, Fr. Augustine Valooran called out my name and said "**Mary**, the Lord is with you. He is taking away all your fears". At that very moment, I felt Jesus' presence in me. The Lord had given me spiritual healing and to date I am free from fears and bad dreams.

MEDITATION

- And our wise Father in heaven knows when we're going to need things too. Don't run out ahead of him." - Corrie ten Boom

- "What wings are to a bird and sails to a ship, so is prayer to the soul." -Corrie ten Boom

- God heals - and He is the great physician and He can heal anyone of any affliction, whether it be physical, mental, emotional, or financial. There are going to be times in your life when you'll need God to heal you or a loved one, so don't be afraid to pray to God for the healing that you need.

- Pray to God for a healing because He hears you. Just remember: God's love heals and it always will.

- If you say, "I want to trust God, but I don't hear Him.", then get near Him to hear Him.

Conversing with God

Most Sacred Heart of Jesus, truly present in the Holy Eucharist, I place my trust in you.

I give you thanks O'Lord with my whole heart. Lord Jesus the true physician and remedy for all ills come and pour your healing on everyone who needs you. I praise and glorify you my God with all the angels and saints

22

GOD'S IDEAL PLAN

"I know the plans I have for you, declares the Lord, plans for welfare and not for evil, to give you a future and a hope."

In everyone's life, there are instances when God intervenes to aid, most unexpectedly in His own mysterious ways. You seek His will with fervent prayers to secure a favour you are craving for but this is declined, much to your disappointment and frustration.

"To reach a port we must sail, sometimes with the wind, and sometimes against it. But we must not drift or lie at anchor. - —Oliver Wendell Holmes

Thomas of Toronto, Canada recounts below God's perfect guidance that led him to live a satisfying life.

My life may not be going the way I planned it; it is going exactly the way God planned.

After retiring prematurely from a staff position in the Sri Lankan Public Service I applied for jobs that suited my qualifications and experience in the African Continent but I did not succeed. I did not even get the favour of an acknowledgement. However, using the influence of someone I knew I applied and attended an interview in Colombo for a good position in Saudi Arabia. I had a reply saying that I was unsuccessful on this occasion and that my CV would be kept on file and passed on to any other clients requiring my services.

I applied locally and secured a good position in a leading mercantile establishment in the city. I was enjoying this position and had earned the trust, confidence and goodwill of my superiors. Two years passed by and I had forgotten about the Saudi Arabian interview. Then out of the blue, I received a letter from a Building Company in Saudi Arabia offering me a good position with attractive emoluments. I could not turn down this offer. I managed to get a release from my Colombo employer and soon arrived in Saudi Arabia. After four years, this company had to close down because of a downturn in the Building Industry in Saudi Arabia but the owner of the Company went out of his way to secure me a better position with a Travel Agency.

I did really well in this travel agency and ended up in one of the highest positions with high emoluments and fringe benefits including almost free air travel. I worked happily for this company for fifteen years but had to leave due to health issues. I had a good innings and was content with what I had achieved.

I firmly believe that it was God's mysterious hands that made me retire early from the Public Service in Sri Lanka, prevented me from going to Africa and guided me to go to Saudi Arabia from where I was able to send my children to study abroad and make the sons settle in the U.K and my wife and daughter in Canada.

MEDITATION

- The heart of man plans his way, but the LORD establishes his steps. - Proverbs 16:9

- Disappointments are just God's way of saying: I've got something better in store.

- When you ask God to direct your path, you have to accept the closed doors as His will, too.

- Having faith in God's timing doesn't come easy to you, either. You have to work really hard at it.

- Don't compare yourself to others. Just go for it. It's all in your head. The good news is, God knows the end result. He is orchestrating something beyond my comprehension right now, and all I have to do is have faith in His timing.

- Don't try to understand everything. Sometimes it is not meant to be understood, just accepted. The more you think, the more excuses you will create for yourself.

- "Don't pray for an easy life. Pray for the strength to endure a difficult one." -Bruce Lee

Conversation with God

Dear Lord Jesus,

I know the plans you have for me are good and not for harm, to give me a future with hope. Thank you for guiding me Lord! Throughout my life you have taken me where I needed to go, to places I didn't even know I wanted to be and to experience the very best you want to give me. I could not have imagined or dreamt of this life you have given me but I know that you planned it and have provided everything I need. Thank you for loving me unconditionally, for giving me not what I want but for giving me what I need. I have hope Lord God for my future in you, for good and not for harm.

Thank you for intervening in my life, for changing my path and taking me in a different direction. Even though at the time I may have felt abandoned thank you for not abandoning me but for bringing me to a better life. Please use me as an instrument to do your will and to help others trust in you and be guided by your love. You have transformed my life and through your mysterious powers have made me into who I am today.

23

A NOVEL SURGERY

"And whatever you ask in prayer, you will receive, if you have faith."

"Ask in faith!"

"So, Jesus answered and said to them, "Have faith in God. For assuredly, I say to you, whoever says to this mountain, 'Be removed and be cast into the sea,' and does not doubt in his heart, but believes that those things he says will be done, he will have whatever he says. Therefore I say to you, whatever things you ask when you pray, believe that you receive them, and you will have them" (Mark 11:22-24).

God's ways are always mysterious. We need to place our trust in Him and He will dispense His mercy without fail.

A new lease of life is a God given opportunity when we become more energetic and active than before:

Thomas of Toronto relates below the story of how God through his mercy relieved him of his fear and anxiety regarding a surgery.

When in Canada, I had a serious ailment and one day I started bleeding heavily through my nose. It was a Sunday. An emergency visit to a Hospital stopped the bleeding but I was advised to see an ENT Specialist the next day. The ENT Specialist referred me to a Cancer Specialist suspecting that it could be cancerous. The agony and desperation my family and I went through is indescribable but I had complete faith in God's mercy. A further confidence was instilled in me when I visited the spiritual healer from Chennai, Fr.Ignatius who placed a Cross on my head, prayed silently and blessed me and said that Jesus had cured me and I would be free of any danger.

I was examined by the specialist and was referred to a Surgeon who confirmed that he had to do a surgery on my face to extract a high concentration of phlegm that had accumulated right from the nose to the skull all over. He was thinking of using ultra high tech methods to avoid disfigurement of my face.

A week later, I underwent surgery in a novel way that left me with only a small mark on top of my right eye. The surgeon told me later that this was the first time he had performed such a surgery and was beaming with triumph and smiles. A biopsy test confirmed that the phlegm accumulation was benign and not malignant.

MEDITATION

- "Whatever you ask for in prayer, believe you have received it and it will be yours." (Mark 11:24)

- "You ask and do not receive, because you ask amiss, that you may spend it on your pleasures" (James 4:3).

- "Now this is the confidence that we have in Him, that if we ask anything according to His will, He hears us. And if we know that He hears us, whatever we ask, we know that we have the petitions that we have asked of Him" (I John 5:14-15)

A Novel Surgery

Conversing with God

Dear Jesus,

Thank you for the faith that you have given me to be able to turn to you in prayer! You are with me always, in times of darkness and times of joy. You always answer my prayers whenever I ask them in faith; even though it might not always be in the ways I had hoped or imagined you are forever faithful.

You have given me a new lease on life and turned something scary and painful into an opportunity to renew my faith and help me to become more energetic and active than ever before.

I give you thanks and praise for your wondrous miracles and deeds. Thank you for sending people into my life to help me and for curing me from my ailments. You set me free from danger and have given me new life. You work in mysterious ways my Lord, ways that are better than mine. I place my trust in you, thank you for your loving mercy that you never fail to pour over us. You work all things together for good. Please help me to be witness to others and to help them see that we need to always place our trust in you. You are faithful and your mercy is without end.

24

"LOST" IN FLORENCE

"I am with you and will watch over you wherever you go, and I will bring you back to this land. I will not leave you until I have done what I have promised you." - Genesis 28:15

Innasi of Toronto, Canada relates his story of how he was saved by prayer when he felt lost in a foreign land..

I joined in a 12-night Europe Mediterranean Cruise- Norwegian Spirit, arranged by the Senior Tamil Centre of Ontario, Canada, commencing 29th May 2014. We "cruised" by air and sea for a spellbound tour, covering five countries: Italy, Turkey, Greece, France and Spain, and twelve cities within them.

On Day 11 (June 9) we were in Florence (Livorno) Italy, walking on cobblestone streets and "discovering" the splendour of the fathers of Italian painting, who lived here, including the works of universal geniuses, Leonardo DaVinci and Michelangelo, including the original statue of David, at the Academia. It was an unforgettable journey through this magnificent city – in both Florence and Pisa – in a day, and standing before its Leaning Tower. While I was absorbing the thrill of viewing the art and culture and taking pictures, I lost track of my group. Our group was led by a guide who was holding a green flag and every one of us was following the green flag. Suddenly, I realised that I was not with our group. I walked for about thirty minutes, to and fro, attempting to talk to anyone for direction, but there was none who understood me – they were all speaking in different tongues. I was beginning to get desperate. I could not even stand in one place as the crowd was "moving" me. While in this situation, I prayed, my Dear Jesus I am lost, I don't know where I am going in this strange place; there is none here who can assist me. Please help me and lead me so that I can regroup with my friends. I recited the Lord's Prayer and prayed the Hail Mary. As I finished the short prayers, I was thinking about the possible consequences of being lost. I could be robbed of my passport and wallet, and I would not be able to identify myself. Just then, someone made me to do a right-about turn and I could feel that someone was "pulling" me forward. I hurriedly walked through storied buildings, through cobblestone streets and moving fast, turning right and left as if I knew the correct way. Suddenly, I saw a few of my friends at a distance. I walked straight into their hands, and they hugged me. Silently, I thanked profusely my dear Jesus and Mother Mary for this "miracle".

MEDITATION

- "Be anxious for nothing, but in everything by prayer and supplication, with thanksgiving, let your requests be made known to God. And the peace of God, which passes all understanding, will keep your hearts and minds through Christ Jesus." - Philippians 4:6,7

- "... He will never leave you nor forsake you. Do not be afraid; do not be discouraged." - Deuteronomy 31:8

- "And when he cometh home, he calleth together his friends and neighbours, saying unto them, Rejoice with me; for I have found my sheep which was lost." - Luke 15:6

- "I am with you and will watch over you wherever you go, and I will bring you back to this land. I will not leave you until I have done what I have promised you." - Genesis 28:15

Conversing with God

Dear Lord, thank you for always guiding me to where I need to go and for taking me to places that I've never been. You are so good and care so much for us your children, you allow us to wander but you also help us when we get lost. I thank you so much for giving me many wonderful opportunities and experiences during my life. I have been given so much and am so grateful for all that you have allowed me to do.

Thank you for never leaving or abandoning me, especially in my times of most need. When I am weak, then you are strong. Thank you for leading me in the right direction, and redirecting my path when I go wrong. You gave us your Mother as an example of how we can give you our yes and how to submit ourselves to your will. Thank you Lord for her and how she leads us closer to you. Throughout my life Lord, you have performed many miracles, I am sorry for not always being grateful or giving you the thanks and praise you deserve. Thank you for continually forgiving me and allowing me to come back to you time and time again.

Amen

25

A FEELING OF GUILT
Missing the Easter Service

Easter is the most important and oldest festival of the Christian Church, celebrating the resurrection of Christ.

Padrupillai of Toronto tells this story of how God punished him for missing the Easter Service.

It was an Easter week-end in Blantyre, Malawi. Our good friends and their families, one a Hindu and the other a Buddhist, decided to visit the cottage inn for the holidays and invited our family to join them. Without a second thought we agreed & set about organising for the trip. Our children were delighted at the very thought of going to the cottage. They love the "cottage trips"

Before driving away, we had to purchase a few items from the super-market. We were in a hurry because we had to be in Zomba at a particular time to meet with another of our Buddhist friends. We rushed to the supermarket to purchase the required items and hurried back to the car. To my surprise I noticed that I hadn't closed the door to the driver's seat properly and I found that my spectacles and various items required for the trip were missing. However, I still had my prescription sunglasses which I was wearing.

We met with our friends at Zomba and we drove away. It was a long drive, and it was soon night-fall. I had a severe problem driving at night with my sunglasses on. I had difficulty focusing and we had to drive at a fairly high speed, in order to reach our destination at the stipulated time. We managed despite my "struggle".

Inwardly, I was not happy and my wife Ida knew it. We have always tried our best to avoid going on picnics and holidays during the Holy Week. I did not show my displeasure to our friends, as they and our children were enjoying the break. Our Hindu and Buddhist friends would not have understood the importance of the Holy Week to a Catholic. So, I did not explain to them my displeasure in missing the Church Services.

All spent the holidays in good spirit, but not I.

On Monday evening we had to return to Blantyre. It was getting dark and I had to drive the entire way wearing my sunglasses and I was driving at 50 km/hr. I requested my pals to speed up and I would call them when we got home.

God had punished for missing the Easter Service and because of this guilty feeling I did not enjoy the Break. At the same time, He has protected me, my family and my friends & their families during our travels.

MEDITATION

- The first Holy Week, by the plan of God, was the most important week in the life of Jesus Christ. This Holy Week, likewise, should be the most important week in the entire year for each one of us. It should be a week of prayer and meditation, in understanding the events of the Passion of Our Lord, knowledge of the Scriptural account of Holy Week is invaluable.

- A day of rest, the Sabbath, was given to us as a gift from God so that we could come into closer relationship with Him. It was not meant to be a mandatory day that we grudgingly go to Church.

- The purpose of the Mass is to give us the opportunity to come into closer relationship with Jesus Christ.

- Take Sunday as the gift from God whereby you can enter more fully into His Scared Heart so that you can experience the love that Jesus truly wishes for you to experience.

- If someone is bedridden and unable to get to Church to receive the Eucharist over a long period of time -- especially during Eastertide -- ask your priest to pay him a sick call.

Conversing with God

Dear Father,

There are so many trials and temptations we face, please continue to guide us and be our example. When we are faced with many options please show us which one you want us to take. When it feels like we can't make the decision we want to make, please give us comfort and refuge. When things go wrong or not to plan, please give me patience and a forgiving heart. Thank you for helping me and guiding me in the past when things didn't' go the way we had hoped. Help me to do good and right, what is pleasing to you and your son Jesus Christ. Without you I can do nothing. Sometimes I find it hard to forgive those who don't understand me or my Christian beliefs. Please help me not to hold grudges but to share about the life you have given me and invite them to know you too. Give me support to be a witness to the faith and share with others the Sacredness of Holy Week and the sacrifice that you made on the cross. You are a mighty saviour and do all things in love. Help me to always be a witness for you and share you unchanging love.

26

CLIMBING THE LADDER OF SUCCESS

"God is the master builder and we are workers"

Gnanarajah of United States of America relates his story of how the good Lord had planned an enviable life path for him.

As a worker in God's vineyard, my aspirations were limited. I wanted only small things in life but He had bigger, broader and better plans for me.

I was not born rich and I had to struggle for everything. God as the master builder had his plans for me. I strongly believe that God guided me every step of the way and made me study, seek and apply for jobs that befitted my ability.

After completing an M.A. in education at Peradeniya University, I was interviewed for a position with UNICEF for a program meant for Estate children. This was to be funded by Switzerland. They wanted a person with a higher degree and research experience who could speak Tamil. I was offered the position after several interviews in Colombo, the final of which was on a Friday afternoon. The UNICEF officials told me that I should wait for the appointment order to be received the following week after approval by the Ministry of Education. This position came with a very attractive salary, a brand new Renault car and a house in Nuwareliya. The appointment order never came. Later I found out that the Deputy Minister wanted her relative to be appointed for the position. The excuse was that I was not born in that area. It was painful news as I had told my family and I was excited about this opportunity.

Not long after this disappointment, I was seconded for service with Palaly Teachers' Training College as a lecturer in Psychology and Science Teaching Methodology. In the meantime I had applied to La Trobe University in Melbourne, Australia for admission to do a Ph.D. They told me that they would not admit me even for a M.A degree. They indicated that I could apply for a M.Ed. degree through course work. When I applied, they wanted my published work in English to assess my fluency in English. I sent my Peradeniya M.A. thesis through airmail post spending a fortune. I did not hear from them for several weeks, and suddenly one day I received a notification from the university offering me admission for Ph.D. on full scholarship with a small travel grant for three years. I was astounded. I completed my studies and this qualification opened many doors for me.

Armed with a Ph.D. I was able to migrate to the USA and get good positions there. I started as a High school coordinator and went on to become the associate superintendent of schools. I was later honoured with the Archbishop of Seattle award for Outstanding Educator of the year. I even established and ran a tuition assistance program to help the needy children to attend Catholic schools irrespective of race or religion.

At the time of my retirement, the fund had increased exponentially from one million to forty million and the Governor of Washington State honoured me by giving me an award for my contribution to multicultural awareness among children of Washington State. All my articles in the national educational magazines were well received and my final article based on research entitled 'Attributes of a quality Catholic School" is widely used by school principals in and outside USA to assess whether their schools meet the criteria for a quality Catholic School.

I never thought I would hold all these positions at National level. These were all the plans of the master builder, my creator, for me. He paved the way for my professional success for which I am ever so grateful.

MEDITATION

- Freedom of choice is something that remains with us. We are free to choose but we are not free from the consequences of our choice.

- We can choose either to obey God or reject His ways. But, having done so, we cannot choose the consequences of our decision.

- We must let God build us as individuals. "God will complete you and make you what you ought to be. He will equip you so that you may carry out His will."

- We may make it work, but only God can make it work right. If it produces frustration, weariness, strife, discouragement, etc. – these are signs that "flesh" is involved.

- "A door of opportunity was opened for Paul." - II Corinthians 2:12. Notice that a door was opened for him; he did not open the door. "A door which no man can shut. " - Revelation 3:7-8

- A word of caution, directed especially to youths. When we are young, we have lots of energy. We can make many varied choices in life. We can make good or bad moral choices. We can mix with the right or wrong crowd. We can go to the places that build our character or to sleazy joints. Yes, we have to make sure that we choose well.

Conversing with God

Dear Lord Jesus,

You have the words of Eternal Life. For I know the plans you have for me Lord - plans for welfare and not for harm - to give me a future with hope. I thank you for directing and guiding me to follow the path you had laid out for me. I thought I knew what I wanted but you know me and love me and so showed your best plans for me.

Throughout my life when different events happened and did not go my way you had a hand in it all and made all things turn out for the better. I praise you and thank you for that. Please help me to continue to stick close to you and walk down the path you have laid out for me. All of my successes in this life would not have been possible without you. I owe all to you; without you I couldn't have climbed the ladder of success. Please use me as an instrument to do your work and help bring others to you. I pray that I may be an example for those who may experience similar hardships to me in their life. Please use me for your work and to help further your kingdom.

You make all things work together for good.

27

DISCIPLINED CHILDREN SHINE IN THEIR ADULT LIFE

"Train up children in the way they should go; even when old they will not depart from it "

Gunaratnam of Toronto is grateful that God had given him good parental guidance during his childhood.

I was privileged to be born in a family that taught their children by deeds rather than by words.

When I was young, I remember my father arriving home (in Jaffna) from Colombo. He didn't go back to work as he had been struck with Parkinson's disease and his hands were constantly shaking. We are thankful that the Lord had been good in helping my father find work in a government department that enabled him to go on early retirement with a pension. We also had a big piece of land with coconut trees, palmyra trees, tamarind trees, and other fruit trees. This enabled us to manage to have a fairly comfortable life.

My parents had five children, two girls and three boys with an age gap of about fifteen years between the first two children and the last three. Anticipating the possibility of worsening health condition, my father decided to build a house so that he could give my oldest sister away in marriage as soon as he could. That he accomplished within two or three years. As he was doing this he was also trying to improve his health by using both western and ayurvedic medicines and succeeded to live long enough to get my oldest sister married, and he was thankful to the Lord for his grace. That must have given him some peace of mind. However his health deteriorated further and he was soon bedridden.

My mother nursed him all by herself. She wouldn't ask us for help. I have seen her saying her prayers at night after my father goes to sleep. Her diligence in saying her prayers demonstrated her faith in God and must have instilled in us our faith.

At 6 pm daily, we used to say the Angelus. There were days when my mother's oldest sister used to come to spend the night in our house. When it was time for bed she would say the Rosary before sleeping.

Thus it can be seen that, the Lord had put in place individuals of faith who acted as role models for us to imitate.

MEDITATION

- The necessity of discipline is to deter destruction

- The means of discipline are actions and words. We bring both words and actions, warnings and consequences, into our children's situations in order to keep them on track.

- The motive in discipline is to express love.

- The goal of discipline is to teach obedience.

- The results of discipline are short-term pain and long-term gain.

Conversing with God

Dear Lord Jesus,

Thank you for everything you have done in my life and for all the people you have placed in my path to help me learn about you. I give you thanks for the role models they have been to me in my life to imitate, as they imitate your love. I could not be who I am without you and your guidance through those you have gifted to me. Although as a child I might not have understood everything that was happening around me, I am thankful for all of my experiences, each one has shaped me into the person that I am today. I know that not everyone has the same opportunities I have been exposed to in my life. Even through the heartache or turmoil I may have been faced with, you have always been faithful to me.

Thank you for the peace and serenity you gave me and my family every time we encountered hardship.

Please help me to be a witness and a role model for my friends, relatives and acquaintances to imitate as I imitate you with my life.

28

HEALING AT OUR LADY MARY'S SHRINE

Catholics regard Mary as the holiest of all the Saints.

Thavapragasam of Brisbane, Australia tells of his experience of supernatural healing.

In the development of a new born child, normally talking and walking happens between 1 – 2 years. In my case, up till the age of 5 years I couldn't talk or walk. This created an enormous anxiety to my parents. A mother naturally yearns to hear her child's first word ''mum'' when the child is a toddler and my mum was deprived of this pleasure. My inactivity further resulted in my putting on weight and my siblings found it difficult to carry me around.

My mum was very worried and wanted my father to take me to the shrine of Our Lady of Madhu. Dad, full of faith, was confident that I would soon start talking and walking. However, at the insistence of my mum I was taken to the shrine of Our Lady on the Feast Day.

During the Eucharistic Elevation at Mass, I was seated on the ground in front of my father who was on his knees. As the priest was raising the Host, dad was bowing down with his eyes closed and suddenly he felt something striking his forehead. When he opened his eyes, to his joy and astonishment he saw me standing; and when the priest raised the Chalice, he was further amazed when I uttered my first word "mum".

The joy and happiness my parents experienced cannot be described in words.

This incident is a perfect example of supernatural healing. I firmly believe that it is the divine intervention through the intercession of Our Lady that I was able to talk and walk at last.

I do not cease to thank God profusely for giving me the gift of speech and mobility, better a bit late than never, which made me the person that I am today.

MEDITATION

- "Lord, have mercy on me," said the blind man.

  "Does thou believe that I can do this?"

  "Yea, Lord, we believe."

  "I can, if ye believe that I can."

- Jesus touched their eyes. That's what they wanted, His hands laid on, He said, "Now, according to your faith, be it unto you." And they had what they said they had. Their eyes come open, and they glorified God..

- How God anointed Jesus of Nazareth with the Holy Spirit and with power. He went about doing good and healing all who were oppressed by the devil, for God was with him. - Acts 10:38

- Then he said to the man, "Stretch out your hand." And the man stretched it out, and it was restored, healthy like the other. - <u>Matthew 12:13</u>

- And Jesus went throughout all Galilee, teaching in their synagogues and proclaiming the gospel of the kingdom and healing every disease and every affliction among the people. So his fame spread throughout all Syria, and they brought him all the sick, those afflicted with various diseases and pains, those oppressed by demons, epileptics, and paralytics, and he healed them. - <u>Matthew 4:23-24</u>

Conversing with God

Dear Lord God,

You are an amazing God who does all things in love. In your timing you grant us all what our heart desires. Thank you Lord Jesus, you are a mighty God who is worthy to be praised.

Thank you Lord for the gift of yourself that you have given to us in the Eucharist. Its power is supernatural. It is a gift to be able to receive you in the Eucharist every time I go to public worship. I am so grateful Lord, that you gave us your mother too, Our Lady. Thank you for your mother who is an example of how we should trust in you and do whatever you tell us. I am forever indebted to you and will trust in you and your divine power always.

29

DREAM COMES TRUE

A dream in its essence signifies the fulfilment of a wish

We are all pilots of our own lives. It is important that we take ownership of leading our lives. God has helped us to reach the station we are currently in. He will guide us to go to where we wish to go in the future if that wish is in line with his plan for our lives.

Nishanthi of Brisbane, Australia talks of a particular dream of hers that became a reality and believes that God has done many marvelous things to her and her family.

My husband and I lived with our three daughters in New Zealand, and we didn't have any relatives close to us. We dreamt that we should go to Australia. I have my sister and aunts, uncles and cousins in Australia. My husband liked the Australian weather and the possibility of a good future for our children. We didn't have any idea how to migrate to Australia. I had my mother with me who had cancer, and my mother- in -law didn't have New Zealand citizenship.

In the meantime, my husband got an offer from work that he could apply for the Brisbane Branch Sales Engineer position. He applied and was successful. I rang my Mother's brother who was willing to help my husband to stay with him for a while until I arrived with my family.

My husband came often to New Zealand and tidied up our home; doing painting, repairs and dealing with agencies to sell the house. My sister called me one day and said that our mother was seriously ill and is in hospital. I went with one of my daughters to see her. I had to leave my other two daughters and my mother-in- law alone and go to Sydney for a couple of days only. I was so disappointed that I couldn't stay with my mum for more days. My mum died shortly afterwards. I took all three daughters this time to Sydney for the funeral and stayed for one week with my sister. We returned to New Zealand, and tried to sell the house but with no luck. My husband visited us in New Zealand several times and did a lot of work on our house.

One day I met one of our friends from our parish and they said they will buy our house, but the agency was not offering it to them. This was because there was already a contract with one buyer and it was to expire only after two weeks. I told them that if that contract fails, then they could buy our house. They were very dedicated members of our church and our house was very close to the church. In the end we sold our house to them.

Our other problem was that I couldn't take my mother in- law to Australia because she had not yet obtained the New Zealand citizenship. We had to make some arrangement for her to stay somewhere before we left for Australia. I asked one of my friends to look after her for one month. In the meantime I also tried to organize for her to go to London and Sri Lanka while waiting for Australian Permanent Resident Visa. It was very kind of my friend to agree to look after my mother- in- law. My Sister-in-law sponsored her for a six month to stay in London. I left my mother in law at my friend's house and they dropped me and my children at the airport to re-join my husband in Australia.

I believe in God; I trusted in Him to make my dream come true. He sent angels in the form of human beings to help realize my dream.

MEDITATION

- Your dream will come to pass in God's time and in God's way.

- The dream of Jesus was to save the world, but when nearing the cross, he asked God if there is any other way to accomplish that apart from the gruesome death on the cross. He however said to God: not my will but yours be done (Luke 22:39-44).

- Dreams take a long time to mature, like a good wine.

Conversing with God

Dear Lord Jesus, you are a wonderful and marvellous God who does all things in love. Thank you for always guiding me and helping me to realise all of my dreams and help make them a reality. Thank you for putting the desires on my heart and providing a way for them to be made manifest in my life. Please continue to align them with your heart and desires. You have made all things work together for good for me Lord. Even when situations seemed desperate you have always remained faithful to me. Thank you for the ability to trust in you constantly and for always being so trustworthy. I am so grateful for all of the angels you have sent my way that have helped me in my life. Please help me to be a witness of my faith and of you to others. Use my life to help others come to know you. You have been so faithful to me. I will always sing of your praises, for you made what seemed impossible possible, you have provided for my family and me and I am eternally grateful. Thank you for allowing us the opportunity to migrate to the lucky country, Australia

30

LOVE, FORGIVENESS AND CHARITY

Make all you can, save all you can and give all you can

Love one another because love comes from God. Whoever loves is a child of God and knows God. Whoever does not love does not know God for God is love. 1 John 4:7-8

"Spread love everywhere you go: first of all in your own house. Give love to your children, to your wife or husband, to a next door neighbour. Let no one ever come to you without leaving better and happier. Be the living expression of God's kindness; kindness in your face, kindness in your eyes, kindness in your smile, kindness in your warm greeting."

-Mother Theresa

Forgiveness is the best form of love. It takes a strong person to say sorry and an even stronger person to forgive.

Forgiving people who have hurt you is your gift to them.

If anyone has the world's goods and sees his brother in need, yet closes his heart against him, how does God's love abide in him? 1 John 3:17

Dr. Ferdinand of Sri Lanka tells how his mentors during school days influenced the way he led the rest of his life.

Two noble ideas were instilled in me in my teenage period; one by my father and the other by Rev. Fr. Long (the unforgettable great principal of St. Patrick's College, Jaffna, Sri Lanka, my school). Both of these ideas greatly influenced my life.

I consider these ideas as God given to me and I endeavoured to apply them to the benefit of the fellow humans I came into contact with throughout my adult life.

My father kept repeating to us a saying in Tamil (our mother tongue) — "A well (source of water) that is regularly drained out will continue to get good fresh water in abundance. A well that is not drained out will stink" — The more you give of your Love, time and talent to others the more you receive all these in greater measure. This has been my experience during the 84 years of my life to date.

Rev. Fr. Long kept repeating to us "Look down on the Sin, yes, but not on the sinner". This attitude has helped me to maintain good relationships with all. I have no one with whom I am angry. Those who caused me anguish are now my good friends because although I was angry with what they did I readily forgave them and they responded with repentance and increased respect and love towards me.

Therefore, if we love, forgive and are charitable towards our neighbour, the Loving God will forgive the million sins we continue to commit through thought, word and deed and shower us with his blessing and love.

Wilfred. F

MEDITATION

- ""Lord, grant that I might not so much seek to

- Be loved as to love – Saint Francis of Assisi

- The things that we love tell us what we are – Saint Thomas Aquinas

- "The proof of love is in the works. Where love exists, it works great things. But when it ceases to act, it ceases to exist – Pope St. Gregory the Great

- "As long as you don't forgive, who and whatever it is, will occupy a rent-free space in your mind." – Isabelle Holland

- "Let us forgive each other – only then will we live in peace." – Leo Nikolaevich Tolstoy

- When you forgive, you in no way change the past – but you sure do change the future." – Bernard Meltzer

- One who is gracious to a poor man lends to the Lord, And he will repay him for his good deed – Proverbs 19:17

- "God has given us two hands, one to receive with and the other to give with." Billy Graham

- "You have not lived today until you have done something for someone who can never repay you." John Bunyan

Conversing with God

Dear Lord Jesus,

I owe all to you; thank you for good mentors who can help me and guide me in my life. Provide such people for me in times of need. Through their influence and witness in my life help me to live a life worthy of my calling and pleasing to you. Thank you that you speak to me through them, and use them as instruments to form me into the person you want me to be.

I am so grateful for my life and all of the opportunities you allow me, and the choices I have the privilege to make. Thank you for the abundance of love you give to me, and the ability to pass that on to others. I receive so much in my life from following your example of giving love, time and talents to others. Thank you for everything you give me and provide to me.

You show me the way and teach me what it means to love the sinner but to hate the sin. Help me to always see people through your eyes and to love them. Show me how to love them like you do.

You have forgiven me all my sins and for which I am forever grateful. Please help me to forgive my neighbor whenever they do something against me. Show me the way, lead and guide me forever. Although I am weak, with you I am strong. With your help I will try not to sin again. Thank you for your endless love and blessings. You are an amazing God.

PROFILES OF A FEW HOLY MEN AND WOMEN

No one lives their life hoping to become a saint. People live a devoted and holy life and spend their time serving God and helping people in need. To be holy means to be free of sin and evil. We can only live a holy life through the power of the Holy Spirit. Sexual purity is an essential requirement for holy living. We must learn to control our own body in a way that is holy and honourable. When we live in obedience to God, we are staying separate from sin and evil.

Saints are people who lived extraordinary lives. Many of those who are made saints have been known to perform miracles during their life time and /or after their death. These powers are given to them by God almighty. Each saint the Catholic Church honours responded to God's invitation to use his or her unique gifts. God calls each one of us to lead a saintly life.

A CALL TO TESTIFY

Each saint has a story and a reason why he or she led an exemplary life.

If we look carefully at the 3000 or so Holy people the Catholic Church has canonised as saints we notice that some spent their lives comforting the sick, fighting against poverty and oppression, some were martyred for spreading the word of God, and others spent most of their life to scholarly study and being recognised as Doctors of the Church.

Whatever the holy men and women did, their lives can be said to be virtuous, selfless and memorable. They were humble and worked to serve God and make a positive difference in the lives of others.

This book highlights briefly the lives of a selected sample of fifteen holy people who are saints and to whom God gave different endowments and through whom he makes his presence known to everyone.

It is amazing that how many of the Holy men and women had to endure life threatening illnesses, humiliation, torture etc. and still worked tirelessly to make God known to the people.

Jesus himself did not want to go to the cross. He asked God 3 times to remove that cup from Him, but He always put God's will first and said "Not my will but thine be done".

It appears to be God's design that some of the holy people including Jesus were meant to live for a short time on this planet and within that time they have had to accomplish a lot to glorify Him.

RECOGNITION AS A SAINT

Men and women who have been devoted Catholic Christians who spent their lives serving God and helping people in need by being selfless and benevolent are recognised as saints generally after a minimum of five years of their death. These saints are required to do at least two miracles before Canonisation. The duration for recognition as a saint i.e. canonisation has taken decades or even centuries in many cases.

Most saints have the following attributes:

purity, righteous, caring, prudent and devout.

The canonisation process starts with a local bishop investigating the candidate's life and sending any information gathered to a panel of theologians in Vatican If the panel approves, then the Pope proclaims that the candidate is venerable.

The next step toward sainthood is beatification which involves proving that the candidate is responsible for a posthumous miracle. Martyrs - those who died for their religious cause - can be beatified without evidence of a miracle.

A second posthumous miracle is usually required before the candidate is canonised as a saint.

31

SAINT AUGUSTINE

Doctor of the Catholic Church

Date of birth: 13 November 354
Place of birth: Tagaste, North Africa
Father's Name: Patricius
Mother's Name: Monica

Augustine, born in 354 AD had an idle childhood and fell into dissipation and sin, a way of life that continued into young adulthood. During this time he fathered a son, Adeodatus, born in 372 AD. Augustine's mother Monica never lost faith, and her earnest prayers saved him from continuing his sinful life.

Augustine studied literature and poetry at the University of Carthage. He pursued a career as a professional public speaker and a teacher of rhetoric. He went to Rome in 383 where he started a school and taught at Milan.

Augustine's Christian life commenced when Bishop Ambrose of Milan made him attend his sermons and convinced him of the truth of Christianity. He began to read the New Testament and the writings of St. Paul. However, his Spiritual, moral and intellectual struggle continued. His main problem was a moral one.

Augustine was converted in September 386 at the age of 32 years. He went back to Tagaste and for three years he lived a life of prayer, study and poverty. .In the year 391 Augustine was ordained as priest.

Augustine established a monastery and delivered numerous sermons. He was consecrated as bishop in 395 which position he held for 35 years. He was made the Director of the Church because of his various writings on the Catholic truth. These included his famous "City of God" and "Confessions".

Augustine died on 28 August 430 at the age of 76 years.

Augustine was canonized in 1303 after popular recognition as a Doctor of the Church.

MEDITATION

- The Bible was composed in such a way that as beginners mature, its meaning grows with them. – *Confessions*

- If you believe what you like in the gospels, and reject what you don't like, it is not the gospel you believe, but yourself. – *Sermons*

- Men go abroad to admire the heights of mountains, the mighty waves of the sea, the broad tides of rivers, the compass of the ocean, and the circuits of the stars, yet pass over the mystery of themselves without a thought. – *Confessions*

- What does love look like? It has the hands to help others. It has the feet to hasten to the poor and needy. It has eyes to see misery and want. It has the ears to hear the sighs and sorrows of men. That is what love looks like.

- What grace is meant to do is to help good people, not to escape their sufferings, but to bear them with a stout heart, with a fortitude that finds its strength in faith. – *City of God*

- Since love grows within you, so beauty grows. For love is the beauty of the soul.

- The world is a book and those who do not travel read only one page.

Conversing with God

Dear Lord,

Please help those who struggle with a particular vice or habit from which they are longing to break away. Render to them the same help the young Augustine got to be converted from his loose living to a life that is pleasing to you. Enable those without belief in Christianity to start believing just the same way as you did for Augustine. Because Augustine cried constantly seeking a changed life, you enabled him by the voice of a child "Take up and Read" and Augustine, while reading a chapter from Paul's letter came across the sentence "Put away all impurity and live in imitation of Jesus" and this made him start a new life.

You made Augustine make up for the sins he committed during his youthful days by practising poverty, supporting the poor and praying with great fervour right up until his death. Please guide each one of us to follow his example.

32

SAINT ANTHONY OF PADUA

Miracle worker

Year of birth: 1195
Place of birth: Lisbon (Now Portugal)
Father's Name: Vicente Martins
Mother's Name: Teresa Pais Taveira
Baptismal name: Fernando

Anthony, whose baptismal name is Ferdinand, born in Lisbon to a wealthy family had a proper early education. At the age of fifteen he joined the Augustinian Abbey of St. Vincent outside of Lisbon, which made him into an intellectual.

Anthony was ordained as a priest at the age of 25. He had the courage to face the ups and downs of life. He loved everyone and was ready to forgive those who did wrong. He was concerned for the needs of others, and had a total trust in God.

Anthony travelled from Portugal to Morocco, to Sicily, to Assisi and finally to a small hermitage In Monte Paola. He also travelled throughout Northern Italy and Southern France preaching. He preached with great learning and fervour.

Anthony went to the city of Rimini where no one was allowed to listen to his sermons. Frustrated, he was walking along Marecchia River where he addressed a different crowd, not people but thousands of fish. This was a miracle indeed!

Anthony was a doctor of the Catholic Church and was a great confessor. He worked miracles, raised the dead to life and helped people to find their lost and stolen articles.

Anthony suffered from dropsy and on 13th June 1231 died at the age of 36. He is believed to have seen Jesus just before his death

MEDITATION

- "Attribute to God every good that you have received. If you take credit for something that does not belong to you, you will be guilty of theft."

- "Damned money! Alas! How many religious did it blind! How many cloistered religious did it deceive! Money is the 'droppings of birds' that blinded the eyes of Tobit."

- «The Life of the Body is the Soul; the Life of the Soul is God.»

- "These symbolize (Proverbs 30:14) the greedy and usurers whose teeth are swords and knifes which they use to devour the poor and steal their magger possessions. All of them are children of this world who consider the children of light to be stupid and believe themselves to be the prudent ones. Their prudence is their death."

- "Christ acts like a loving mother. To induce us to follow Him, He gives us Himself as an example and promises us a reward in His kingdom."

- "Anyone, then, who desires to live chastely in Christ Jesus, must flee not only the mouse of lust, but even from its very scent."

- "The spirit of humility is sweeter than honey, and those who nourish themselves with this honey produce sweet fruit»

- "Solicitude for material things distracts the soul and divides it. The devil seizes the divided soul and drags it to hell."

Conversing with God

Dear Lord,

Anthony is one of those you molded into a great preacher and one of the young saints. Although you planned to keep him in this world for only a short period, you gave him the opportunity to serve you and spread your name in many parts of the world within that time.

We honour St. Anthony as the Doctor of the Catholic Church and a great confessor. He is well known for his work to help the poor and for his obedience to his superiors.

You gave him the power and authority to do many miracles. You made him to do wonders for the afflicted and those who reached for his help. He had a great love for you and for your creation.

Please help me especially to imitate the ways of St. Anthony by practicing interior as well as exterior mortification. Help me also to have the courage St. Anthony had to face the ups and downs of my life, to love everyone and have concern for the needs of others and be ready to forgive those who do wrong to me.

33

SAINT FRANCIS OF ASSISI

The first stigmatic

Year of birth: 1181
Place of birth: Assisi, Italy
Father's Name: Pica de Bourlemont,
Mother's Name: Pietro Bernardone dei Moriconi

Born in Assisi, Italy Francis was a spoilt lad till he was 14 years. He indulged in fine food, booze and women. He was good at archery, wrestling and horsemanship .He spent a year in prison after fighting in a battle between Assisi and Perugia.

Francis started turning to God at the age of 20 years. After the release from prison, he heard voices of Jesus asking him to repair the Christian church and to live a life of poverty. He received a vision one day that left him with the stigmata of Christ i.e. the wounds resembling that of the crucified Christ.

Francis lived a life of humility, poverty and simplicity. He started teaching a new kind of emotional and personal Christian religion that everyday people could understand. He often retreated to remote places to pray and contemplate alone with God. He did not merely learn the he Bible but obeyed its commandments.

Francis cared for the sick. Though he was terrified of their disease, he visited the lepers and cared for them. His heart reached out to the poor and the rejected of society, to bring to them the love of Christ.

Francis wished that people be generous, and willing to use their material wealth cheerfully and without compulsion for the furthering of God's divine will. He lived what he preached. This is a welcome challenge to the spiritual lives of today's Christians.

Francis died on October 3, 1226, at the age of 45, in Assisi, Italy. He was canonised as a saint just two years after his death, on July 16, 1228.

MEDITATION

- "It would be considered a theft on our part if we didn't give to someone in greater need than we are."

- "I should be accounted a thief by the great Almsgiver were I to withhold that which I wear from him who has greater need of it than I." (St. Francis of Assisi)

- "If we can enter the church day and night and implore God to hear our prayers, how careful we should be to hear and grant the petitions of our neighbours in need."

- "Each one should confidently make known his need to the other, so that he might find what he needs and minister to him. And each one should love and care for his brother in all those things in which God will give him grace, as a mother loves and cares for her son."

- "Let us, therefore, have charity and humility and give alms because it washes the stains of our sins from our clothes. For people lose everything they leave behind in this world; but they carry with them the rewards of charity and the alms which they gave, for which they will have a reward and a just retribution from the Lord."

- "Poverty is the way to salvation, the nurse of humility, and the root of perfection. Its fruits are hidden, but they multiply themselves infinite ways."

- "My brother, when thou seest a poor man, behold in him a mirror of the Lord, and of His poor Mother. In the sick, in like manner, consider that He bore our sicknesses."

- "We should have no more use or regard for money in any of its forms than we have for dust. Those who think it is worth more, or who are greedy for it, expose themselves to the danger of being deceived by the devil."

- "If we had any possessions, we would be forced to have arms to protect them, since possessions are a cause of disputes and strife, and in many ways we would be hindered from loving God and our neighbour. Therefore in this life we wish to have no temporal possessions."

- "We can never know how patient or humble someone is when everything is going well with him. But when those who should cooperate with him do exactly the opposite, then we can know. A man has as much patience and humility as he has then, and no more.

- "'Blessed are the poor in spirit, for the kingdom of heaven is theirs (Mt. 5:3).' There are many who, applying themselves insistently to prayer and good deeds, engage in much abstinence and many mortifications of their bodies, but they are scandalized and quickly roused to anger by a single word which seems injurious to their person, or by some other things which might be taken from them. These are not poor in spirit because a person who is truly poor in spirit hates himself (cf. Lk. 14:26) and loves those who strike him on the cheek (cf. Mt. 5:39)."

Conversing with God

Dear Lord,

You made Francis, the pleasure loving handsome young man, at the age of 20 years to revolt against his wealthy silk merchant father to serve you, after telling him "hereto I have called you my father on earth but now on I would only say "Our father who art in heaven".

Further, you made him change his life by a voice "Go Francis and repair my house which as you see is falling into ruin".

Please give the same instruction to the youngsters of today so that they can spread your name in some way even if they can't do things like Francis. Encourage them to live a life of poverty, helping the poor and the rejected of society, to bring your love into their hearts.

34

SAINT PHILIP NERI

(The apostle of Rome)

Date of birth: 21 July 1515
Place of birth: Florence, Italy
Father's Name: Francesco di Neri
Mother's Name: Lucrezia da Mosciano.

Philip received his early education at <u>Dominican</u> monastery in Florence. He was sent to his uncle Romolo at the age of 18, to assist him in his business.

Philip had a religious conversion within a short time thereafter and he no longer cared for things of the world and went to Rome. He worked as a tutor for two years in Rome in the house of a Florentine aristocrat named Galeotto Caccia.

Philip pursued his own studies for a period of three years under the guidance of the <u>Augustinians</u> after which he worked amongst the sick and the poor and also ministered to the prostitutes of the city.

For seventeen years Philip lived as a layman in Rome converting people primarily through preaching the Gospel, teaching of the catholic doctrine and the practice of frequent confession. He made friends with people, loved them, and drew them into the heart of Christ precisely through love. Philip sought God by helping the neighbour. He also had a profound love for the mother of God

Philip was ordained as a priest on 23 May 1551. He died at the age of 80 years, on 25 May 1595, and was canonised as a saint in 1622.

MEDITATION

- Cast yourself into the arms of God and be very sure that if he wants anything of you, He will fit you for the work and give you strength.

- The best remedy for dryness of spirit, is to picture ourselves as beggars in the presence of God.

- An excellent method of preserving ourselves from relapsing into serious faults, is to say every evening, "Tomorrow I may be dead."

Conversing with God

Dear Lord,

You made Philip to grow up as a dutiful and cheerful lad. At the age of 18 years you changed his life through giving him a mystical experience. Thereafter he began to spend a lot of time in prayers eating frugal meals. You made him to draw the people towards you by showing love.

Please help me to show the same sort of love Philip had to my neighbours and others whom I associate with, and draw them to you.

35

SAINT IGNATIUS OF LOYALA

(The Founder of the Jesuits)

Year of birth: 1491
Place of birth: Spain
Father's Name: Don Beltran
Mother's Name: Marina

Ignatius was born as the youngest son of a noble and wealthy couple. He was an expert dancer, a swordsman and a womaniser. He became a page and then a soldier of Spain to fight against the French. Unfortunately he had to end his military career because of a series of operations.

Ignatius read the lives of the saints, and decided to dedicate himself to becoming a soldier of the Catholic Faith. He travelled and studied in different schools, finished in Paris, where he received his degree at the age of 43. He is famous for his book on "Spiritual Exercises"

Ignatius was hated by many because of his humble lifestyle. Despite this, he attracted several followers at the university, including St. Francis Xavier, and soon started his order called The Society of Jesus, or Jesuits.

Ignatius died suddenly on 31 July 1556 at the age of 65 and was canonised on March 12, 1622.

MEDITATION

- "If our church is not marked by caring for the poor, the oppressed, the hungry, we are guilty of heresy".

- Act as if everything depended on you; trust as if everything depended on God."

- The safest and most suitable form of penance seems to be that which causes pain in the flesh but does not penetrate to the bones, that is, which causes suffering but not sickness".

- God is no blind moneychanger; he values love's works more than its words.

- If God makes you suffer greatly, it is a sign that he wants to make you a great saint.

- A good life is much better than learning, whether for obtaining or for communicating to others the gifts of the Holy Spirit.

Conversing with God

Dear Lord,
You called your faithful servant Ignatius of Loyola to a life of the most exalted sanctity in the very close imitation of Jesus.

Please help us also to be your soldiers following his example. Help us to defend our faith and teach others about you. Use us as you used Ignatius. Help us to be a witness and to lead others closer to you. Ignatius taught us about Spiritual Exercises. Help us to use them to discern the plans you have for us.

We know that Ignatius was not always a man of faith but through your work in his life he was able to become a warrior. We know that you can do all things. Please work in our lives and help us to be warriors of the faith. As Ignatius was hated, we know we might be too. Please help us to have the same strength he did to persevere and move on.

36

SAINT RITA OF CASCIA

Saint of the impossible

Year of birth: 1381
Place of birth: Roccaporena, near Spoleto, Italy
Father's Name: Antonio Lotti
Mother's Name: Amata Lotti

Rita was married at the age of twelve to a cruel and harsh man. She spent eighteen extremely unhappy years and was widowed when her husband was killed in a brawl. Her two sons also died and Rita wanted to become a nun but was refused because of the requirement that all nuns should be virgins.

Like other saintly women Rita suffered greatly in an unhappy marriage. Her patience and forgiveness were exemplary and eventually brought about the conversion of her erring spouse. Her holiness was reflected in each phase of her life.

Starting at the age of thirty-six Rita spent forty years giving herself whole heartedly to charity, striving especially to preserve peace and harmony among the citizens of Cascia.

When Rita was about sixty years she had an external sign (on the forehead) of stigmatization and union with the Lord. During the last four years of her life she was confined to bed.

Rita died on May 22, 1457 and was canonized on May 24, 1900. At her canonization ceremony, she was bestowed the title of Patroness of Impossible Causes, while in many countries, Rita came to be known as patroness for abused wives and heartbroken women.

MEDITATION

- **"God is the teacher of the Prophets, the co-traveller** with the Apostles, the power of the Martyrs, the inspiration of the Fathers and Teachers, the perfection of all saints."

- God gave us faculties for our use; each of them will receive its proper reward. Then do not let us try to charm them to sleep, but permit them to do their work until divinely called to something higher.

- <u>There are more tears shed over answered prayers than over unanswered prayers.</u>

- The tree that is beside the running water is fresher and gives more fruit.

Conversing with God

Dear Lord

Please give me the patience that was modelled by St. Rita. Help me to forgive even in the most difficult of circumstances. Make me follow Rita's footsteps and persevere on always giving myself to you. Help me promote peace and harmony wherever I go and show others that there is another way to live. Although Rita faced many difficulties she continued to whole-heartedly devote herself to charitable activities. From her example please help me to get inspired to give generously. Please help me to never give up but always try my best to stick to whatever good work I start. Although confined to bed during her final years on earth Rita was able to cling on to her faith. Encourage me to follow her example and never forsake you.

37

SAINT PATRICK

(Apostle of Ireland)

Year of Birth: 387 AD
Place of Birth: Great Britain (Kilpatrick, near Dumbarton, in Scotland)
Father's Name: Calpurnius
Mother's Name: Conchessa.

St. Patrick of Ireland, one of the world's most popular saints is the son of a wealthy tax collector. When Patrick was sixteen years old he was captured and taken to Ireland as a slave. During the six years of slavery, he turned to God **in prayer. After six years, he escaped and sailed on a boat back to his family in Britain.**

Patrick had a dream in which the people of Ireland **were calling out to him «We beg you, holy youth, to come and walk among us once more.»**

Patrick went to France where he studied for the priesthood. He was ordained a priest and within a few years, a bishop.

Patrick preached the Gospel throughout Ireland for forty years, converting many. He converted wealthy women, some of whom became nuns in the face of family opposition. He also dealt with the sons of kings, converting them too.

Patrick used the shamrock to explain the Trinity. He worked many miracles and wrote of his love for <u>God</u> **in** "Confessions". The absence of <u>snakes</u> in Ireland gave rise to the legend that they had all been banished by St. Patrick.

St Patrick is believed to have died on March 17 in 461AD

 Patrick was never canonized. The reason is he lived in the 5th century and the process we now know as canonization did not exist until centuries later. Patrick was the first major figure to reject slavery and for that alone he is recognised as a saint.

MEDITATION

- I am Patrick, yes a sinner and indeed untaught; yet I am established here in Ireland where I profess myself bishop. I am certain in my heart that "all that I am," I have received from God. I am imperfect in many things, nevertheless I want my brethren and kinsfolk to know my nature so that they may be able to perceive my soul's desire.

- For some time I have thought of writing, but I have hesitated until now, for truly, I feared to expose myself to the criticism of men, because I have not studied like others, who have assimilated both Law and the Holy Scriptures equally and have never changed their idiom since their infancy, but instead were always learning it increasingly, to perfection, while my idiom and language have been translated into a foreign tongue.

- I am, then, first of all, countryfied, an exile, evidently unlearned, one who is not able to see into the future, but I know for certain, that before I was humbled I was like a stone lying in deep mire, and he that is mighty

151

came and in his mercy raised me up and, indeed, lifted me high up and placed me on top of the wall. And from there I ought to shout out in gratitude to the Lord for his great favours in this world and for ever, that the mind of man cannot measure.

- The Lord took pity on me thousands upon thousands of times, because he saw within me that I was prepared, but that I was ignorant of what to do in view of my situation; because many were trying to prevent this mission. They were talking among themselves behind my back, and saying: 'Why is this fellow throwing himself into danger among enemies who know not God?' Not from malice, but having no liking for it; likewise, as I myself can testify, they perceived my rusticity. And I was not quick to recognize the grace that was then in me; I now know that I should have done so earlier.

Conversing with God

Thank you for the example of St Patrick

O' God, you shaped. Patrick to teach and save the people of his time and place. You filled him with great faith and a burning desire to work hard for your Kingdom. Please grant me also a lively faith and a strong will to live my life to build your Kingdom where I live.

Please help me to always turn to you in prayer even when difficulties arise. St Patrick was so young when he was captured as a slave, yet gave his life for so many. At every age give me the strength to choose to rely not on my own strength but to place my trust in you.

Help me to reach out to many for you and bring them to your love. May you work through me as you worked through St Patrick and convert the hearts of many. In difficult circumstances I pray for wisdom to know which way to go and to speak the words those I am ministering too need to hear. Help me to stand up for the rights of all especially those caught in slavery as St Patrick did.

38

LOUIS AND ZELIE MARTIN

The parents of St Teresa

Year of Birth: Louis - 1823
Zelie - 1831
Place of Birth: Louis – Bordeux, France
Zelie – Saint-Denissur-Sarthon, France
Father's Name:
Mother's Name:

Louis was the third of five children of Pierre-François Martin and Marie-Anne-Fanny Boureau. All Louis' siblings died before reaching age 30. Louis intended to become a monk, but was rejected because he did not succeed at learning Latin. He become a watchmaker.

Zelie was the second daughter of Isidore Guérin and Louise-Jeanne Macé. Zélie wanted to become a nun, but was turned away by the Sisters of Charity of Saint Vincent de Paul due to respiratory difficulties and recurrent headaches.

Zelie fell in love with the watchmaker Louis and married him. Zélie had a successful business and so Louis sold his watchmaking business and entered into partnership with her

Zelie gave birth to nine children, five of whom entered religious life. The couple lived modestly, reached out to the poor and the needy, and led daily prayers in the household.

Zelie Martin died of breast cancer In 1877, at age 45 and Louis died in 1894 after suffering greatly. .Louis and Zelie' Martin were canonised on 18th October 2015.

MEDITATION

- In a Christian marriage spouses strive to lead each other to holiness. Louis and Zelie Martin show how a marriage not only benefits the couple, but their children, the Church and society.

- The conjugal love of Louis and Zelie is a pure reflection of Christ's love for his Church, but it is also a pure reflection of the "resplendent love without stain or wrinkle, but holy and immaculate" (Ep 5, 27) as the Church loves its Spouse, Christ.

- Studies have found the old adage, "Couples that pray together, stay together" to be true. Prayer reinforces the connection between couples and as a result, their marriages are strengthened!

- Prayer encourages unity. As we come before God as a couple, we are coming as a team and reminding ourselves that we are on the same side. When we offer our prayers to God together we are naturally aligning our hearts as couples for one shared hope and outcome.

- Prayer promotes emotional intimacy. The tender moments that are created when our hearts are open and vulnerable to each other grow our love and level of intimacy in our relationship.

- Praying together cannot help but change our marriages for the better.

Conversing with God

Dear God,

You gave us Louis and Zélie Martin, the parents of St. Therese, as an example of holiness in marriage. They remained faithful to you and your commandments in all the duties and trials of life. They desired to raise their children to become Holy and may their example help Christian family life to blossom in our world today.

Louis and Zellie Martin lived out their vocation to the sacrament of marriage and gave us a wonderful example to follow. Please help us to take their lead and live out our vocation with the same zeal. Though they lived modestly they still reached out to the poor and needy; please help me to do the same and never forget my brothers and sisters, no matter where I may find myself in life.Though I may face pain and suffering please help me to persevere and stay faithful to you always like your servants Louis and Zelie Martin.

39

SAINT PADRE PIO

'In the spiritual life, he who does not advance goes backwards.'

Date of birth: 25 May 1887
Place of birth: Pietrelcina, Italy
Father's Name: Grazio Mario Forgione
Mother's Name: Maria Guiseppa de Nunzio

Forgione family attended daily Mass, prayed the Rosary nightly and fasted three days a week. Padre Pio was attracted to church, prayer and hymns starting from the age of 5 years. He is known to have conversed with Jesus and suffered attack by devil during his younger days.

Padre Pio had a desire to be a priest since 1897. He also wanted to be a Friar. He acquired the necessary qualifications and at the age of 15, took the Habit of the Order of Friars Minor and was called Fra (for brother) until his priestly ordination in 1910.

Padre Pio got the wounds of Christ, the stigmata within a month of his ordination after Jesus and Mary appeared to him while he was praying.

He is remembered as "a great apostle of the confessional"

Padre Pio was famous for his healings. He died on 23 September 1968, and was canonised on 16 June 2002.

MEDITATION

- Do not allow the sad spectacle of human injustice to disturb your soul.

- Jesus speaks of nothing but love, and gives us perpetual proof of his love.

- God will not allow you to be lost if you persist in your determination not to lose him

Conversing with God

Dear Lord, you helped Padre Pio to live a life of charity, self-sacrifice and selfless love. You made him a pastor of the Church to feed your sheep with his word and to teach them by his example. Guide us to live our lives by his holy example and by doing so glorify your blessed name.

Not everyone has the privilege to attend daily Mass and pray the Rosary nightly with their family. You blessed Padre Pio with that gift from a young age. Please help me to follow his example and when possible attend daily Mass and pray the Rosary. Help me to follow the example of Padre Pio and not be afraid to converse with Jesus every day even if it means I may be susceptible to attacks from the devil. Please help me to persevere and put my relationship with you above anything else. Lord God you gave Padre Pio the desire and graces to accept your calling on his life to the Priesthood. Please give me the graces and desires to say yes to whatever vocation you place on my heart. Thank you for the gift of Padre Pio and the witness he is to us here on earth. May we place our trust in you like he did from a young age.

40

SAINT THOMAS AQUINAS

Year of birth: 1225
Place of birth: Roccasecca, Italy
Father's Name: Landulph
Mother's Name: Theodora

Thomas Aquinas is an authority of the Roman Catholic Church and a prolific writer He was one of the greatest theological thinkers of the 13th century. He is the foremost classical proponent of natural theology, and the father of the Thomistic school of philosophy and theology.

Thomas was sent to monastery to train among Benedictine monks when he was just 5 years old. He remained at the monastery until he was 13 years old, when the political climate forced him to return to Naples.

Thomas spent the next five years completing his primary education at a Benedictine house in Naples. He also attended the University of Naples.

Thomas secretly joined an order of Dominican monks in 1243 His family kidnapped him and held him captive for an entire year and attempted to deprogram him of his new beliefs. However, he held fast to his ideas and went back to the Dominican order following his release in 1245.He continued to pursue his studies with the Dominicans in Naples, Paris and Cologne.

Thomas was ordained in Cologne, Germany, in 1250. He taught theology at the University of Paris and later earned his doctorate in theology under Professor St. Albert the great.

St. Thomas died on 7 March 1274. He was canonised on July 18, 1323 and was proclaimed a Doctor of the Church in 1567

MEDITATION

(Some Quotes of Saint Thomas Aquinas)

- A man has free choice to the extent that he is rational.

- Better to illuminate than merely to shine, to deliver to others contemplated truths than merely to contemplate.

- By nature all men are equal in liberty, but not in other endowments.

- Faith has to do with things that are not seen and hope with things that are not at hand.

- How can we live in harmony? First we need to know we are all madly in love with the same God.

- It is necessary for the relaxation of the mind that we make use, from time to time, of playful deeds and jokes

- The things that we love tell us what we are.

- Three things are necessary for the salvation of man: to know what he ought to believe; to know what he ought to desire; and to know what he ought to do.

- To one who has faith, no explanation is necessary. To one without faith, no explanation is possible.

Conversing with God

Dear God, you called Thomas to spend his life in academic pursuits making him a professor of theology and a teacher You ordained that Thomas should enlighten your Church, through his scholarly studies. Please help us to understand and practice what he taught and become better Christians.

41

SAINT ALOYSIUS GONZAGA (LUIGI)

The Patron Saint of All Students

Date of Birth: 9 March, 1568
Place of Birth: Northern Italy
Father's Name: Ferrante Gonzaga
Mother's Name: Marta Tana di Santena

Aloysius was born the eldest of seven children. He was sent to a military camp at the age of five to get started on his career. So he grew up among violence and brutality. Later he was sent to Florence in 1576, at the age of 8, to receive further education. He distinguished himself, not only in philosophy, but also in theology.

Aloysius, while he was ill, took the opportunity to read about the saints and to spend much of his time in prayer.

After reading a book about Jesuit missionaries in India, Aloysius felt strongly that he wanted to become a missionary himself. Although Aloysius wanted to become a priest, several members of his family worked hard to persuade him to change his mind.

In 1585 Aloysius was accepted as a Jesuit novice. He successfully completed his studies. Aloysius fell ill with a disease of the kidneys in 1590 which was to trouble him throughout his life. He received a vision in which he was told that he would die within an year.

When a plague broke out in Rome in 1591, he volunteered to work with plague victims, but unfortunately he himself contracted the disease in March. He received the <u>Sacrament of the Anointing of the Sick</u> and recovered, but, as he was told in another vision, he died on 21 June 1591.

Aloysius was canonised in 1726 and named Patron of All Students in 1729.

MEDITATION

- It is better to be the child of God than king of the whole world.

- There is no more evident sign that anyone is a saint than to see him leading a good life and at the same time a prey to desolation, suffering, and trials.

- He who wishes to love God does not truly love Him if he has not an ardent and constant desire to suffer for His sake.

Conversing with God

Dear God

You put young Aloysius on earth to live in an age of corruption and licentiousness and enabled him to counteract this libertineness with acts of penance. You also gave him the opportunity to grow in maturity in the Jesuit Order. He was filled with fervour for the ill that he sacrificed himself in service to them. Please grant us the privilege to follow Aloysius in his innocence and imitate him in penitence

42

SAINT BERNADETTE

Date of birth: 7 January 1844
Place of birth: Boly, Mill, Lourdes
Father's Name: Francois Soubirous
Mother's Name: Louise Casterot

Bernadette's family struggled for living during her childhood. When Bernadette was ten, cholera scourged Lourdes, taking her to death's door, and leaving her with asthma and palpitations of the heart.

Bernadette's poor health and the family's financial problems often forced her to live with relatives and friends. Bernadette worked as a shepherdess.

Bernadette saw eighteen visions of Virgin Mary in a grotto over a five month period, the first one was on 11 February 1858 when she was out with two of her companions gathering twigs and sticks for the fire

Bernadette's visions and the messages she received from the "Lady" were difficult to believe by the local church authorities although the people of Lourdes in general believed her. Bernadette was given messages of prayer and penitence to share with the world. She was asked by the "Lady" to drink water that was bubbling from the ground, as well as wash in it. She was also asked to eat the herb from the ground.

The Grotto soon became a place of prayer, of gathering and of devotion. People who drank the water and bathed in it experienced cures for their illnesses. She was asked by the "Lady" to speak to the priests and build a chapel at the Grotto.

Bernadette joined the Congregation of the Sisters of Charity of Nevers in 1866 and became known as Marie-Bernarde. Despite her poor health, Bernadette was content with her life as a nun.

Bernadette could not get along with the novice-mistress at the convent and was subject to painful humiliations.

Bernadette died on 16 April 1879. Her body was exhumed three times and since 1925 her incorrupt body has been in a shrine in the Chapel of the Convent of St.Gildard, in Nevers.

Bernadette was canonised as a Saint in 1933.

MEDITATION

- "Nothing is anything more to me; everything is nothing to me, but Jesus: neither things nor persons, neither ideas nor emotions, neither honour nor sufferings. Jesus is for me honour, delight, heart and soul."

- "Those who are humble of heart will be glorified. How beautiful the heavenly crown will be for those who are genuinely humble despite outward humiliations, those who follow the humility of the Saviour in every way."

- **"Love overcomes, love delights, Those who love the Sacred Heart rejoice!"**

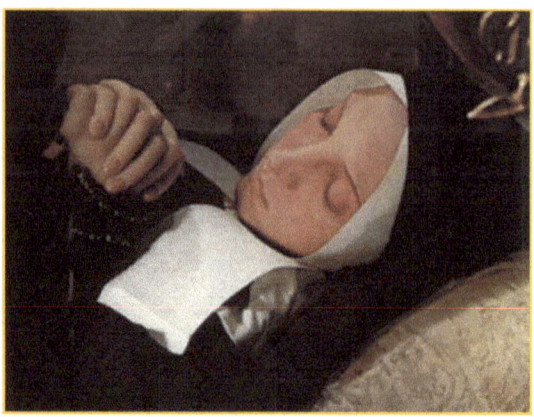

St. Bernadette's incorrupt body

Conversing with God

Dear God, You chose Bernadette, to give us the Miraculous waters of Spiritual and physical healing at Lourdes. Please help us to follow Bernadette's example and always be mindful of the needs of others, especially those whose sufferings are greater than ours.

43

SAINT TERESA OF AVILA

Originator of Carmelite Reform

Date of birth: 28 March 1515
Place of birth: Avila, Spain
Father's Name: Don Alonso Sanchez de Capeda
Mother's Name: Dona Beatriz Davila Ahumada

Teresa is a great mystic and the first woman Doctor of the Catholic Church. She entered the Carmelite Convent in 1535 but unfortunately within three years she became an invalid.

Teresa underwent a religious awakening in 1555. She opened the first St. Joseph's convent of the Carmelite Reform. She also established sixteen more convents and nurtured them throughout Spain.

Teresa was a great writer and her writings on the progress of Christian soul towards God are recognised masterpieces.

Teresa died on 4th October 1582 at the age of 67. She was canonised a saint on 12 March 1622.

MEDITATION

- "We need no wings to go in search of God, but have only to find a place where we can be alone and look upon Him present within us."

- "Mental prayer in my opinion is nothing else than an intimate sharing between friends; it means taking time frequently to be alone with Him who we know loves us."

- "Never compare one person with another: comparisons are odious."

Conversing with God

O God, you filled the heart of. Teresa with the treasures of your divine love; grant that, like her, we may love you and suffer all things for you.

You chose Teresa to show the Church the way to seek perfection, grant that we may always be nourished by the food of her heavenly teaching and fired with longing for true holiness.

44

SAINT MARY MACKILLOP

Cofounder of the Josephites Order

Date of birth: 15th January 1842
Place of birth: Brunswick Street, Fitzroy, Melbourne
Father's Name: Alexander Mackillop
Mother's Name: Flora McDonald

Mary's father was her teacher and educator. At the age of eight years Mary cared for her five younger brothers and sisters who regarded her as their second mother. Mary joined the work force at the age of 16 years and helped her large family.

Mary not only excelled as a teacher but also as a horsewoman having inherited the skill from her mother. Her traits included kindness, patience, maturity beyond her years, an instinctive compassion and selflessness.

Mary guided the Josephites Order to establish schools for the poor and underprivileged in South Australia first and later across Victoria and Sydney

Despite resentment from general public and the Australia's Irish born bishops to what Mary was trying to achieve, God helped her to succeed in her vision of creating a better world for all. She provided Catholic education to the poor, the underprivileged children and the indigent.

Mary worked independently without being under the control of the Bishop and other Church leaders which upset them. She was excommunicated, for insubordination for resisting Bishop Sheil's attempt to bring her under control. She travelled to Rome in 1873 seeking Papal approval for the Order, in which she partly succeeded. The final approval was given in 1888.

Bishop Sheil realised his error, retracted his statements and Mary's membership of the Church was restored.

Mary Mackillop, Mother Mary of the Cross, died on Sunday 8 August, 1909 after a long illness.

Mary Mackillop was canonised on 17 October 2010.

MEDITATION

- "Remember we are but travellers here."

- "We must teach more by example than by word."

- "God gives me strength for what is necessary"

Conversing with God

Dear God, You gave Mary Mackillop the power to recognise when the poor were being used and abused, and the strength to work for the dignity and equality of all people. You made her to speak out in society when the opinion of women mattered little. You empowered her to work for you despite her poor health and unpleasant opposition to her ways of doing things. Please grant me also the courage to stand up against injustice and face life's challenges with hope.

45

SAINT MONICA

Patroness of married women

Year of birth: 332 AD
Place of birth: Tagaste, Northern Africa
Father's Name: unknown

Mother's Name: unknown

Born in North Africa, Monica grew as a good Christian. However her parents got her married to Patricius, a pagan. Although Patricius admired Monica, he was very cruel to her. Monica never complained about him to anyone. Instead she prayed for him fervently. Patricius became a Christian in 371, one year before his death

While Monica was elated with her husband's good death, she was sad that her 19 year old son Augustine was living a bad and, a selfish life and had turned to a false religion. Monica prayed fervently to change his way of life. After years of prayers her reward came when he was converted. He changed not only as a good Christian but became a priest, a bishop and a great writer.

St. Monica died in Ostia, outside Rome, in 387 at the age of 56 years with her son Augustine at her bedside.

MEDITATION

- "Nothing is far from God."

- "Pray with great confidence, with confidence based upon the goodness and infinite generosity of God and upon the promises of Jesus Christ. God is a spring of living water which flows unceasingly into the hearts of those who pray."

- "You cannot be half a saint; you must be a whole saint or no saint at all."

Conversing with God

Dear God, you gave us Monica as an example of how tearful prayers and fasting can bring about conversion to Christ of those dear ones who lead unchristian lives. When loved ones reject the Church help us to pray Like St. Monica!

Please grant that we might have in us, like Monica the faith so that we may live all our years in serenity.

MOTHER THERESA

The saint of the gutters

Year of birth: 1929
Place of birth: Albania
Father's Name: unknown
Mother's Name: unknown

Mother Teresa was the **founder of the Order of the Missionaries of Charity**, a Roman Catholic congregation of women dedicated to helping the poor.

Mother Teresa, an Albanian-Indian, was a famous as the Catholic nun. She dedicated her life to caring for the destitute and dying in the slums of Kolkata. In 1979 she received the Nobel Peace Prize and after her death at 87 years due to cardiac arrest was canonised as Saint Teresa on 4 September 2016.

POPE JOHN PAUL II

Year of birth: 1920
Place of birth: Wadowice
Father's Name: Karol Kaczorowska
Mother's Name: Emilia Kaczorowska

Pope John Paul was a great scholar and great apostle of Christ. He is remembered for **his successful efforts to end communism**, as well as for building bridges with peoples of other faiths, and issuing the Catholic Church's first apology for its actions during World War II.

John Paul II died at the age of **84** in April 2005. He was declared a saint in 2014 alongside Pope John XXIII at a ceremony in the Vatican.